asian food

asian food

simple recipes for delicious food every day

RPS

RYLAND PETERS & SMALL
LONDON • NEW YORK

Designer Paul Stradling

Senior Editor Miriam Catley

Production Controller Gary Hayes

Art Director Leslie Harrington

Editorial Director Julia Charles

Indexer Hilary Bird

First published in 2014 by
Ryland Peters & Small
20–21 Jockey's Fields
London WC1R 4BW
and
519 Broadway, 5th Floor
New York NY 10012

www.rylandpeters.com

Text © Valerie Aikman-Smith, Nadia
Arumugam, Ghillie Basan, Vatcharin
Bhumichitr, Jordan Bourke, Tori Finch,
Manisha Gambhir Harkins, Brian Glover,
Dan May, Jennie Shapter and Ryland Peters
& Small 2014

Design and photographs © Ryland Peters
& Small 2014

ISBN: 978-1-84975-502-3

10 9 8 7 6 5 4 3 2 1

A CIP record for this book is available from
the British Library.

US Library of Congress Cataloging-in-
Publication data has been applied for.

Printed and bound in China

notes

• All spoon measurements are level, unless
otherwise specified.

• All herbs used in these recipes are fresh, unless
otherwise specified.

• All fruit and vegetables should be washed
thoroughly before consumption. Unwaxed citrus
fruits should be used whenever possible.

• The recipes in this book are given in both metric
and imperial measurements. However, the
spellings are primarily British and this includes
terminology relating to chilli peppers. British 'chilli'
and 'chillies' are used where Americans would
use 'chile', chili and 'chiles'.

• Regular soy sauce often contains wheat
products: if you prefer wheat-free ingredients, use
Japanese tamari soy sauce.

• It is advisable to wear food-safe vinyl gloves
when preparing chillies – no matter how diligently
you wash your hands there will always be some
lingering spice on your fingers.

contents

introduction

Fresh, tasty and bursting with nutritious ingredients and lively flavours, the food of East Asia has never been more popular. This collection of aromatic and sizzling hot recipes is a must for any lover of more exotic and adventurous food. Whether you need inspiration for appetizers and fingerfoods for sharing with drinks, speedy weekday dishes or something more impressive for entertaining you'll find the perfect recipe here.

Cooking classic and contemporary dishes from East Asia is easier than you might think. The following recipes have been written to be used by people cooking in a Western kitchen using ingredients widely available in supermarkets and Asian stores. In the first chapter, Small Bites, Thai fish cakes are surprisingly simple to make and taste delicious served with dipping sauces. Soups are a staple and recipes include Miso and Wakame Soup with Japanese Seven-Spice. For a weekday meal in minutes try the refreshing Laotian Pork and Glass Noodle Salad, punchy Indonesian Fried Rice or simple yet elegant Japanese Noodles with Gomadare Sesame Seed Sauce. Finally, for a more substantial and satisfying dish the Main Dishes include Quick-Fried Teriyaki Salmon, Burmese Pork Hinleh or Sweet and Sour Pork with Pineapple and Cucumber.

You do not need any specialist equipment but a few essentials will help you on your way. A pestle and mortar is useful for pounding fresh herbs and spices and a wok or a large, heavy-based frying pan/skillet is invaluable for stir-frying. Finally, a slotted spoon and a stack of paper towels will come in handy for some of the deep-fried dishes.

Asian food is the modern way to eat well every day and this essential collection of recipes provides all the inspiration you need.

pastes and rubs

Asian pastes and rubs add heat and spice to any meat, chicken or fish dish and can be used as a marinade or added to a dipping sauce. Wonderfully vibrant, these pastes and rubs are well worth trying at home and can be stored and used again.

Szechuan rub

The Chinese province of Szechuan is known for cooking with fiery chillis and salty condiments. Wonderful dishes come out of this area and this simple rub is perfect to keep on hand.

1 tablespoon Szechuan peppercorns
1 tablespoon dried chilli/red pepper flakes
1 teaspoon chilli powder
1 teaspoon dried garlic powder
1 teaspoon ground ginger
1 teaspoon coarse sea salt
1 teaspoon black peppercorns

Makes 3½ tablespoons/scant ¼ cup

Put all the ingredients into an electric spice grinder and process to a coarse powder.

Store the rub in a glass jar with a tight-fitting lid for up to 6 months.

Fermented black bean paste

Fermented black beans are used extensively in Asian cooking and give a deep salty flavour to any dish. They taste great and look even better. Add them to a dipping sauce or blend in a marinade.

45 g/⅓ cup Chinese fermented black beans
2 small Thai chillies, finely chopped
1 garlic clove, finely chopped
1 tablespoon freshly grated ginger
2 tablespoons toasted sesame oil
4 tablespoons/¼ cup kecap manis (Indonesian soy sauce)

Makes 120 ml/½ cup

Put all the ingredients in a bowl and mix together.

Store the paste in an airtight container in the fridge for up to 2 weeks, or you can also freeze it for up to 6 months.

Thai lemongrass paste

This is a wonderful, fresh-tasting paste that works really well with poultry. The vibrant aromas of lemongrass, lime leaves and lemon fill the air.

a 5-cm/2-inch piece of galangal or ginger, peeled and roughly chopped
2 stalks fresh lemongrass, bashed and roughly chopped
6 Kaffir lime leaves
4 birds' eye chillies, roughly chopped
2 tablespoons honey
2 tablespoons fish sauce
1 teaspoon Sriracha sauce or hot sauce
freshly squeezed juice and grated zest of 2 limes
3 tablespoons vegetable oil
a large bunch of coriander/cilantro, chopped

Makes 240 ml/1 cup

Put all the ingredients in a blender or food processor and process to a thick paste.

Store the paste in an airtight container in the fridge for up to 1 week.

Laksa paste

The essential spice paste for Laksa Lemak, one of the great soups of Southeast Asia – a speciality of the Chinese-Malay Nonya community of Singapore.

6 shallots, coarsely chopped

4 red chillies, deseeded and chopped

1 stalk of lemongrass, outer leaves discarded, the remainder very finely chopped

1 teaspoon ground turmeric

1 garlic clove, chopped

½ teaspoon ground ginger or galangal

a tiny piece of shrimp paste, toasted in a dry frying pan/skillet or hot oven, or ½ teaspoon anchovy paste

6 macadamia nuts or 12 almonds

1 kaffir lime leaf (optional)

2 tablespoons Thai fish sauce

Makes about 75 ml/⅓ cup

Using a blender or mortar and pestle, grind all the ingredients to a thick, chunky paste. If using a blender, add a little water to let the blades run.

Thai red curry paste

This paste is fierce in colour and heat. Decrease or increase the chillies according to taste.

8–10 red bird's eye chillies, deseeded and chopped

a small piece of dried shrimp paste, toasted in a dry frying pan/skillet or in a hot oven, or 1 teaspoon anchovy paste plus a dash of Thai fish sauce

1 tablespoon grated kaffir lime or regular lime zest

1 stalk of lemongrass, outer leaves discarded, remainder very finely chopped

1 teaspoon cumin seeds, toasted in a dry frying pan/skillet

1 teaspoon white or black peppercorns

1 tablespoon coriander/cilantro seeds, toasted in a dry frying pan/skillet

2–3 garlic cloves, chopped

a 3-cm/1-inch piece of fresh galangal or ginger, peeled and chopped

3 tablespoons chopped shallots or onions

1–2 tablespoons finely chopped coriander/cilantro root

Makes about 150 ml/⅔ cup

Using a blender or mortar and pestle, grind all the ingredients to a thick, chunky paste. If using a blender, add a little water to let the blades run.

Thai green curry paste

This mild paste is made from spices and herbs; if you wish to be true to its roots, feel free to use many more chillies.

1 tablespoon grated kaffir lime zest or regular lime zest

4–5 green bird's eye chillies, deseeded and chopped

several lemon balm leaves (optional), chopped

1 stalk of lemongrass, outer leaves discarded, the remainder very finely chopped

¾ teaspoon coriander/cilantro seeds, toasted in a dry frying pan/skillet

a handful of coriander/cilantro leaves, chopped

a handful of coriander/cilantro stems and roots, chopped

2–3 garlic cloves, chopped

2 spring onions/scallions, chopped

a 3-cm/1-inch piece of fresh galangal or ginger, peeled and chopped

3 tablespoons Thai fish sauce

Makes about 120 ml/½ cup

Using a blender or mortar and pestle, grind all the ingredients to a thick, chunky paste. If using a blender, add a little water to let the blades run.

condiments and seasonings

There is an incredible array of condiments and seasonings available in Asian cooking. Here are just a few of the classics and you will find many more recipes to accompany the dishes throughout the book.

Indonesian sambal

This is just one of the huge family of fiery Indonesian condiments. The number of chillies may sound daunting, but deseeding reduces their heat. Use fewer chillies if you prefer or, if you like fiery foods, use bird's eyes instead.

15 red chillies, deseeded and chopped
2 tomatoes, halved
10 small shallots, preferably pink Thai
8 cashew nuts
2 garlic cloves, chopped
a 3-cm/1-inch piece of fresh galangal or ginger, peeled and chopped
a small piece of dried shrimp paste, toasted in a dry frying pan/skillet or hot oven
1 tablespoon brown sugar
3 tablespoons peanut oil
2 tablespoons freshly squeezed lemon juice
salt, to taste

Makes about 175 ml/scant ¾ cup

Using a blender or mortar and pestle, grind all the ingredients to a paste. Serve as a condiment.

Peanut sauce

This versatile sauce can be used as an accompaniment to dishes such as satay and other grilled meat.

250 g/2 cups shelled raw peanuts
2 fresh red chillies, deseeded and thinly sliced
2 fresh bird's eye chillies, deseeded and thinly sliced
1 onion, finely chopped
1 garlic clove, crushed
1 teaspoon sea salt
2 teaspoons brown sugar
200 ml/¾ cup canned coconut milk

Makes about 375 ml/1½ cups

Toast the peanuts in a dry frying pan/skillet set over a low heat. Transfer to a clean, dry paper towel, rub off the skins, then put the nuts in a blender. Grind to a coarse meal, then add the chillies, onion, garlic, salt, sugar and coconut milk. Blend to a purée, then transfer to a saucepan and cook over medium heat, stirring, until thickened.

When ready to serve, thin with water until it reaches your desired consistency.

Chinese five-spice powder

This essential Chinese blend is made with a minimum of five spices – the first five are listed below – but some blends may also contain extras spices such as ground ginger or coriander. It should be very fragrant, with star anise dominating.

1 teaspoon Szechuan peppercorns, black seeds discarded
1 whole star anise
¾ teaspoon fennel seeds
½ teaspoon whole cloves (about 10)
2 pieces cinnamon stick or cassia bark, about 5 cm/2 inches long
¼ teaspoon ground ginger

Makes about 1 tablespoon

Put the Szechuan peppercorns into a dry frying pan/skillet and toast briefly. Using a spice grinder or mortar and pestle, grind the peppercorns, star anise, fennel seeds, cloves and cinnamon, then stir in the ground ginger. Store in an airtight container.

Szechuan seasoning

Easy to make, this spiced and toasted Chinese salt seasoning is used to sprinkle over foods. It is also excellent as a dip for dim sum snack foods and other party foods.

1 teaspoon coarse salt
½ tablespoon Szechuan peppercorns
1 teaspoon Chinese five-spice powder

Makes 2½ teaspoons

Put the salt and Szechuan peppercorns into a dry frying pan/skillet and toast gently until both begin to brown (take care because they burn easily). Remove from the heat, let cool, grind to a powder and mix in the five-spice powder.

Japanese wasabi paste

Wasabi paste is available in tubes. It is often a bright lime green colour. The colour changes after opening, so don't keep opened tubes longer than a few days. Aficionados prefer to use powder, and the finest quality is very pale indeed. Serve with sushi and sashimi.

1 tablespoon wasabi powder

Makes 1 tablespoon

Put the powder into a small bowl, add a dash of water and stir with a chopstick.

Wasabi cream

Wasabi a perfect way to dress something up, especially cream. Serve alongside sushi. You could also try adding it to a simple mayonnaise (see page 26) and serve with tempura.

2 tablespoons wasabi powder
240 ml/1 cup crème fraîche
sea salt and ground black pepper

Makes 240 ml/1 cup

Whisk together the wasabi powder and crème fraîche in a glass bowl and season with the salt and pepper.

Store in a glass container with a tight fitting-lid in the refrigerator for up to 1 week.

Japanese gomasio

A delicious seasoning that can be sprinkled over most foods (as long as they are not already salty). The toasted sesame flavour is superb.

2 teaspoons black sesame seeds
½ teaspoon coarse salt

Makes about 1 tablespoon

Toast the sesame seeds in a dry frying pan/skillet until aromatic. Grind the salt and sesame seeds to a powder and store in an airtight container.

Japanese shichimi togarashi

A ubiquitous Japanese spice mix, widely available in supermarkets. This blend of seven spices includes the unusual flavours of sansho, yuzo (dried citrus peel) and nori (dried seaweed). Sprinkle over soups. Sometimes other seeds like hemp or rape are used, as well as shisho herb.

½ teaspoon white or black poppy seeds
½ teaspoon black sesame seeds
1 teaspoon white sesame seeds
1 teaspoon chilli powder
1½–2 teaspoons ground sansho
1½ teaspoons dried yuzo flakes
few pieces of nori or mixed dried sea vegetables such as dulse and sea lettuce

Makes about 2 tablespoons

Put all the ingredients into an airtight container, stir well, then store in a cool, dark place.

Nam Prik Pao

Whether this is actually a cooking paste, a condiment, a dip or even a jam is a matter of conjecture, but it clearly illustrates the flexibility of the flavours and the many uses to which Nam Prik Pao lends itself. It is delicious with rice, noodles, vegetables, fish and meat.

120 ml/½ cup vegetable oil
3 large shallots, chopped
3 garlic cloves, chopped
a pinch of sea salt
3 Thai chillies, deseeded and chopped
½ teaspoon shrimp paste (gapi)
2 tablespoons ground dried shrimp
1½ tablespoons fish sauce, or to taste
2 teaspoons palm sugar, or to taste
1 teaspoon tamarind paste, or to taste

Makes about 200 ml/¾ cup

Heat a small wok over medium heat and add 2 tablespoons of the oil. Fry the shallots and garlic for 5 minutes, or until softened and translucent. Put them into a mortar and pound with a pestle into a smooth paste. Add the salt and chillies and repeat the process. Add the shrimp paste and dried shrimp. Continue pounding until you have a fine, uniform paste. Put the remaining oil in the wok and heat over medium heat. Reduce the heat and add the paste. Fry gently to allow the ingredients to combine their flavours. Season with the fish sauce, palm sugar and tamarind paste to taste. Mix well and remove from the heat. Store in an airtight sterilized container in the fridge.

Japanese pickled ginger

A favourite accompaniment for sushi and sashimi, this is available in larger supermarkets and Asian stores.

a 10-cm/4-inch piece of fresh ginger, peeled and thinly sliced with a mandoline
a pinch of sea salt
6 tablespoons Japanese rice vinegar
1 tablespoon sugar
sterilized preserving jar with seal or glass jar with tight fitting lid

Makes 120 ml/½ cup

Put the ginger and salt into a small bowl and toss well. Mix the vinegar, sugar and water in a bowl, pour over the ginger and mix again. Transfer to the sterilized jar, covering the ginger with the liquid. Seal and refrigerate for at least 3 days, or up to 1 week.

dressings

Asians dressing range from the delicate Japanese dressings served over beautifully arranged small salad bowls to the more complex dressings from Thailand and Vietnam comprising hot, salt, sour and sweet elements.

Nihai-zu

This is a simple dressing for shellfish and fish salads.

3 tablespoons white rice vinegar
2 tablespoons tamari soy sauce
a pinch of sea salt
Makes about 75 ml/⅓ cup

Put all the ingredients in a bowl and whisk with a fork until combined.

Goma-zu

This sesame seed dressing is good with raw vegetables.

4 tablespoons black sesame seeds
1 tablespoon sugar
2 tablespoons tamari soy sauce
1 tablespoon sake
2 tablespoons rice vinegar
Makes about 200 ml/¾ cup

Toast the sesame seeds in a dry frying pan/skillet set over low heat until aromatic. Using a mortar and pestle, grind to a powder. Add the sugar and grind again, then stir in the soy sauce, sake and vinegar. If preferred, add 1 tablespoon water or dashi.

Kimi-zu

A Japanese version of mayonnaise.

2 egg yolks
½ teaspoon sea salt
1½ tablespoons white sugar
½ teaspoon cornflour/cornstarch
4 tablespoons dashi stock
2 tablespoons rice vinegar
Makes about 200 ml/¾ cup

Put the egg yolks in a heatproof bowl set over a saucepan of simmering water. Don't let the base of the bowl touch the water. Whisk well, then beat in the salt, sugar and cornflour/starch. Gradually stir in the dashi and vinegar. Continue simmering, stirring until thickened. The cornflour/starch will stop it curdling, but don't let it boil.

Ponzu sauce

This fashionable dressing can be difficult to make because yuzu fruit (a kind of citrus fruit) is rare outside Japan. The juice is sometimes available in specialist stores, or can be ordered.

grated zest and juice of 1 yuzu or small blood orange
tamari soy sauce

Put the grated zest and juice in a bowl, then stir in an equal quantity of soy sauce.

Sambai-zu

This is a popular everyday Japanese salad dressing, used in many homes. Sweet, salty and sour.

3 tablespoons rice vinegar
1 teaspoon tamari soy sauce
1 tablespoon white sugar
a pinch of sea salt
Makes about 75 ml/⅓ cup

Put all the ingredients in a bowl and beat with a fork until combined.

Vietnamese chilli-lime dressing

You will notice that there is quite a lot of brown sugar in this dressing, because of the large quantity of chilli and ginger.

6 tablespoons freshly squeezed lime juice
1 tablespoon Vietnamese fish sauce
2 tablespoons brown sugar
2 fresh red or green chillies, deseeded and very finely chopped
1 garlic clove, crushed
a 3-cm/1¼-inch piece of fresh ginger, peeled and grated
Makes about 200 ml/¾ cup

Put all the ingredients in a small bowl and beat with a fork until the sugar has dissolved.

Sesame oil dressing

Serve poured over a simple chicken dish to elevate your meal to new heights.

a 3-cm/1¼-inch piece of fresh ginger, peeled and sliced
3 spring onions/scallions, chopped
1 fresh red chilli, deseeded and chopped
1 tablespoon Szechuan peppercorns
200 ml/¾ cup peanut oil
4 tablespoons sesame oil
Makes about 375 ml/1½ cups

Put the ginger, spring onions/scallions, chilli and peppercorns in a small blender and pulse to chop. Put the peanut and sesame oils in a saucepan and heat until hot but not smoking. Remove from the heat, add the flavourings, stir, cover with a lid, let cool, then strain.

Lime dressing

This tangy lime dressing works well drizzled over a Thai mango beef salad.

1 tablespoon Thai fish sauce
freshly squeezed juice of 1 lime
1 teaspoon brown sugar
Makes about 60 ml/¼ cup

Mix in a small bowl and serve as a dipping sauce, or sprinkled over an Asian-style salad.

Spicy Thai dressing

A classic Thai combination of salt, sour, sweet and hot elements.

4 tablespoons Thai fish sauce
freshly squeezed juice of 1 lemon or 2 limes
2 teaspoons brown sugar
2 tablespoons red Thai curry paste
Makes about 125 ml/½ cup

Put the fish sauce, lime or lemon juice, sugar and curry paste in a bowl and beat with a fork until combined.

Thai fresh chilli dressing

This dressing packs a powerful punch.

4 tablespoons freshly squeezed lime juice
2 tablespoons Thai fish sauce
2 fresh red or green chillies, deseeded and very finely chopped
Makes about 125 ml/½ cup

Put the lime juice, fish sauce and chillies in a bowl and stir with a spoon until combined.

dipping sauces

Served alongside some of the most irresistible small bites, dipping sauces can also be used as sauces for spooning over rice or other dishes.

Vietnamese tamarind dip

This South-east Asian dip has a wonderful sour flavour that can only come from tamarind. You could also use this as a dressing.

75 g/3 oz. lump tamarind or 1 teaspoon tamarind paste
2 teaspoons peanut oil
1–2 teaspoons Vietnamese/Thai fish sauce
1 large garlic clove, crushed
1 teaspoon jaggery (unrefined palm sugar) or brown sugar
a dash of fresh lime juice (optional)

Makes about 2 tablespoons

To prepare the lump tamarind, put it into a small bowl. Add 200 ml/¾ cup hot water and let soak for 15 minutes. Squeeze the tamarind through your fingers in the water and continue until all of it has been squeezed into a pulp. Press through a sieve.

Put 3 tablespoons of the prepared tamarind, or the 1 teaspoon paste into a small bowl, whisk in the peanut oil and fish sauce, add the garlic and jaggery and stir until dissolved. Add a dash of lime juice if using, then serve.

Nuóc Cham (Vietnamese-style dipping sauce)

Vietnamese cuisine is one of the most interesting and diverse in the world. Nuóc Cham and its variations are now perhaps its most universally available sauce and are added as required to virtually any savoury dish. It is particularly good when drizzled over rice dishes or as a dip for vegetable tempura (see left).

1 small lime
3 garlic cloves, crushed
2 small hot green chillies, deseeded and finely chopped
4 teaspoons unrefined golden caster sugar or raw cane sugar
60 ml/¼ cup Vietnamese-style fish sauce

Makes about 150 ml/²⁄₃ cup

Squeeze the juice from the lime into a small bowl and set aside. Scrape the pulp from the lime and grind it, along with the garlic and chillies, with a pestle and mortar to form a paste. If you find it difficult to get a paste, the ingredients could be briefly pulsed in a food processor. Add 75 ml/⅓ cup water and the sugar to the bowl of lime juice and stir until the sugar has dissolved. Scrape the chilli paste into the bowl, add the fish sauce and mix.

Variation: Add the finely chopped chillies to the bowl at the end if you prefer not to grind them into the Nuóc Cham.

Note: Vietnamese fish sauce is lighter in style than traditional Nam Pla (Thai fish sauce). If you are unable to source this, Thai-style fish sauce still works well but you may wish to reduce the quantity slightly or add to taste.

Soy and ginger dipping sauce

This simple dipping sauce is perfect served with Chinese dim sum.

3 tablespoons light soy sauce
3 tablespoons Chinese rice wine or dry sherry
a 1-cm/½-inch piece of fresh ginger, peeled and sliced

Makes about 90 ml/generous ⅓ cup

Put all the ingredients in a small bowl and beat with a fork until the sugar has dissolved.

From delicate Vietnamese summer rolls packed with fresh herbs to crispy
Japanese tempura the wonderful array of bite-size morsels of Southeast Asia
are perfect served as appetizers, snacks or offered as fingerfood at parties.

small bites

spicy tofu satay with soy dipping sauce

300 g/10 oz. tofu, rinsed, drained, patted dry and cut into bite-size cubes

leaves from a small bunch of fresh basil, shredded, to serve

sesame oil, for frying

Marinade

3 lemongrass stalks, trimmed and finely chopped

1 tablespoon peanut oil

3 tablespoons soy sauce

1–2 fresh red chillies, deseeded and finely chopped

2 garlic cloves, crushed

1 teaspoon ground turmeric

2 teaspoons sugar

sea salt

Soy dipping sauce

4–5 tablespoons soy sauce

1–2 tablespoons Thai fish sauce

freshly squeezed juice of 1 lime

1–2 teaspoons sugar

1 fresh red chilli, deseeded and finely chopped

a packet of wooden or bamboo skewers, soaked in water before use

Serves 3–4

Here is a very tasty dish that does wonderful things to tofu, which can be rather bland. Full of the flavours of Southeast Asia, this Vietnamese dish is sold at street stalls as a snack but serve it as an appetizer or with noodles as a main dish.

To make the marinade, mix the lemongrass, peanut oil, soy sauce, chilli, garlic and turmeric with the sugar until it has dissolved. Add a little salt to taste and toss in the tofu, making sure it is well coated. Leave to marinate for 1 hour.

Prepare the soy dipping sauce by whisking all the ingredients together. Set aside until ready to serve.

To cook the tofu, you can stir-fry the cubes in a wok with a little sesame oil and then thread them onto sticks to serve, or you can skewer them and grill them over charcoal or under a conventional grill/broiler for 2–3 minutes on each side. Serve the tofu hot, garnished with the shredded basil and with the dipping sauce on the side.

These dumplings are called potstickers because of the technique of first pan-frying their bottoms, then pouring over stock, quickly covering and letting them steam in the resulting hot vapour.

vegetable potstickers

300 g/3 cups finely shredded red cabbage

1 teaspoon sea salt flakes

2 tablespoons vegetable oil, plus about 65 ml/¼ cup for shallow-frying

1 tablespoon finely grated fresh ginger

4 garlic cloves, finely chopped

1 small carrot, grated

1 tablespoon light soy sauce

18 gow gee wrappers

125 ml/½ cup vegetable stock

4 spring onions/scallions, thinly sliced

1 handful of roughly chopped fresh coriander/cilantro

freshly ground black pepper

Orange dipping sauce

65 ml/¼ cup light soy sauce

65 ml/¼ cup rice vinegar

65 ml/¼ cup freshly squeezed orange juice

Makes 18 small dumplings

To make the dipping sauce, put all of the ingredients in a bowl and whisk to combine. Cover and set aside until ready to serve.

Put the cabbage in a bowl and sprinkle over the sea salt. Cover and let sit for 30 minutes, stirring a few times. Put the cabbage in a colander and squeeze out as much liquid as possible. Tip it onto a chopping board and finely chop. Transfer to a bowl and set aside.

Put the 2 tablespoons oil in a large frying pan/skillet or wok and set over high heat. Add the ginger and garlic and stir-fry for just a few seconds to soften the ingredients and flavour the oil. Add the cabbage and carrot and stir-fry for 1 minute. Add the soy sauce and season with black pepper. Transfer to a bowl and let cool.

Put 2 teaspoons of the mixture in the centre of a gow gee wrapper. Brush around the edges with a little water and bring the two sides together to form a half-moon shape, snugly enclosing the filling. Press the edges firmly and crimp or pleat around the edges to seal. Gently tap the dumplings on their base so that they get a flattened bottom. Put the dumplings on a baking sheet lined with parchment paper, cover and refrigerate until you are ready to cook them.

Cook the potstickers in 2 batches. Put half of the oil for shallow-frying in a non-stick frying pan/skillet and set over medium heat. Add the first batch of potstickers to the pan and cook for 2–3 minutes until the bottoms sizzle in the oil and turn crisp. Shake the pan while they are cooking so that they don't stick. Carefully add half of the stock, standing well back from the pan, as it will splutter. Quickly cover with a lid and let cook for 2–3 minutes, until the filling is cooked through. Cook the second batch in the same way. Sprinkle with coriander/cilantro and spring onions/scallions and serve warm.

This wheat-free version of tempura is made using rice and cornflour/cornstarch. It's important to get the temperature of the oil just right to avoid burning the batter before the vegetables and prawns/shrimp inside are cooked through.

tempura vegetables and prawns

selection of vegetables, eg., carrot, sweet potato, aubergine/eggplant, squash, broccoli, (bell) pepper, spring onion/scallion, beet(root)

600 ml/2½ cups vegetable, sunflower or rapeseed oil

4 king prawns/jumbo shrimp, shells and central veins removed, but tails on

100 g/¾ cup rice flour, plus extra for coating

100 g/¾ cup cornflour/cornstarch

1 teaspoon baking powder

small bottle of ice-cold sparkling water

2 egg whites

few cubes of ice

sea salt and freshly ground black pepper

Wasabi mayonnaise

300 ml/1¼ cups extra virgin oil

300 ml/1¼ cups sunflower oil

2 egg yolks

squeeze of lemon juice

3 teaspoons wasabi powder or paste

Serves 4

To make the mayonnaise combine the oils in a jug/pitcher. Put the egg yolks, wasabi, lemon juice and a pinch of salt in a mixing bowl. Start to whisk and very slowly feed the oils in to the mixing bowl a little at a time until the mixture begins to emulsify. Once you have added all the oil, stir in the wasabi powder or paste and refrigerate.

Cut the hard vegetables into thin slices about ½ cm/¼ inch thick. Cut softer vegetables such as aubergine/eggplant, spring onion/scallion or (bell) pepper a little thicker.

If you have a deep fat fryer, heat the oil to 190°C/375°F, otherwise heat it in a deep saucepan. If you don't have a cooking thermometer, check the temperature by dropping a breadcrumb into the oil. It should turn golden in about 25–30 seconds. While the oil is heating, mix together the flours, baking powder, ½ teaspoon salt and a good pinch of pepper in a bowl. Slowly stir in just enough cold sparkling water until you have a yogurt consistency, but don't over-whisk. Using an electric whisk, beat the egg whites in a separate bowl until they form hard peaks. Fold the eggs into the batter, stir the ice cubes through to keep it cold.

Lightly coat the vegetables and prawns/shrimp in rice flour. Shake off any excess, then dip into the batter. Carefully place them into the hot oil. Don't overcrowd the fryer or pan, as it will bring down the temperature of the oil. The prawns/shrimp will take about 3 minutes and the vegetables about 2 minutes. Remove the tempura with a slotted spoon and drain on paper towels.

prawns wrapped in crispy noodles

1 egg

½ teaspoon salt

½ teaspoon sugar

1½ teaspoons freshly ground white pepper

8 king prawns/jumbo shrimp, peeled and deveined, tails on

1 nest fresh ba mee noodles (see note)

peanut or sunflower oil, for deep-frying

Sweet and hot sauce

4 tablespoons sugar

6 tablespoons rice vinegar

½ teaspoon salt

2 small red chillies, finely chopped

an electric deep-fryer (optional)

Serves 4

Prawns/shrimp wrapped in crispy noodles produce a delicious combination – the contrast between the softness of the prawns/shrimp and the crisp texture of deep-fried noodles is exceptional. Though this dish looks spectacular, it is not difficult to make. In fact, it's a recipe for the home cook, because it has to be wrapped and fried at the last minute, and doesn't lend itself to the large quantities and advance preparation methods of restaurant chefs.

To make the sauce, put the sugar, vinegar and salt in a saucepan and heat, stirring until the sugar dissolves. Add the chillies and 4 tablespoons water, stir well and simmer until it becomes a thin syrup. Pour into a dipping bowl.

Put the egg, salt, sugar and pepper in a bowl and beat well. Add the prawns/shrimp and mix well. Lift 3–4 strands of noodle and wrap each prawn/shrimp, winding the strands into a mesh thickly covering the prawn/shrimp.

Fill a wok or deep-fryer one-third full with the oil or to the manufacturer's recommended level. Heat until a scrap of noodle will puff up immediately.

Working in batches if necessary, fry the wrapped prawns/shrimp until golden brown. Drain and serve with the sweet and hot sauce.

Note Ba mee noodles are made from egg and wheat flour and are always sold fresh in 'nests'. Buy them in Chinese or South-east Asian markets.

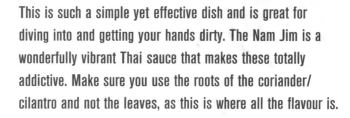

This is such a simple yet effective dish and is great for diving into and getting your hands dirty. The Nam Jim is a wonderfully vibrant Thai sauce that makes these totally addictive. Make sure you use the roots of the coriander/cilantro and not the leaves, as this is where all the flavour is.

8 king prawns/jumbo shrimp, shell on

Nam jim

roots of 1 bunch of coriander/cilantro

2 garlic cloves

a 2.5-cm/1-inch piece of fresh ginger

1 large red chilli, deseeded, plus extra slices, to serve

1 tablespoon coconut palm sugar

sea salt

2 teaspoons fish sauce

juice of 1 lime

Serves 3–4

charred prawns with nam jim

Using a pestle and mortar, pound the coriander/cilantro roots, garlic, ginger and chilli until you get a paste. This will take a few minutes of fairly aggressive pounding! The skin of the chilli will also come loose so when that happens, you should pick it out and discard it.

Add the sugar and pound, then add a little salt, the fish sauce and lime juice. Mix together and taste. This Nam Jim is so full of flavour that it should almost sing out at you, with each ingredient holding its own. Adjust it slightly until you get the right balance.

Heat a stovetop grill pan over high heat. Cut the prawns/shrimp lengthways down the middle of the belly, so you have nice long halves. Place them, flesh side down, on the dry pan, cook for 2 minutes, then flip them over and cook for another 2 minutes.

Once cooked, tangle the prawns/shrimp together on a plate with some coriander/cilantro leaves and extra chilli slices scattered over. Drizzle with Nam Jim and serve.

steamed prawns stuffed with chilli jam

South-east Asian chilli pastes are complex and delicious. You'll need lots of hot towels to mop up spicy fingers after eating this hands-on dish.

3–5 prawns/shrimp per person, depending on size, unpeeled and uncooked

4 tablespoons mirin, Shaohsing (rice wine) or dry sherry

freshly squeezed juice of 1 lime, plus 3 extra limes, halved, to serve

Chilli jam

125 g/4 oz. dried shrimp

8 garlic cloves, unpeeled

10 pink Thai shallots, or 2 regular

2 tablespoons peanut oil

12 large dried red chillies, medium hot, broken in half and deseeded

1 tablespoon tamarind paste

2 tablespoons brown sugar

1 tablespoon fish sauce

Serves 4

To make the chilli jam, put the dried prawns/shrimp onto a piece of aluminum foil and crumple up the edges. Put onto a baking sheet. Add the garlic and shallots and transfer to a preheated oven and cook at 200°C (400°F) Gas 6 until dark brown and aromatic, about 30 minutes. Remove the prawns/shrimp from their sheet of foil after 10 minutes.

Put 1 tablespoon of the oil into a small frying pan/skillet, add the chillies and stir-fry for a few seconds to release the aromas. Grind to a meal with a mortar and pestle or in a blender, then add the prawns/shrimp and grind again. Add the garlic and shallots and grind again. Put the tamarind paste into a small bowl and stir in 2 tablespoons water, the sugar and fish sauce.

Add the remaining 1 tablespoon oil to the frying pan/skillet, add the chilli mixture and heat until aromatic. Stir in the tamarind mixture and cook until thick. Set aside until cool enough to handle. Store any leftover mixture in the refrigerator for up to 3 days.

Cut down the backs of the unshelled prawns/shrimp and remove the vein. Press the chilli jam into the back cut, pushing it between the shell and flesh as much as possible. Put onto a plate in a steamer, sprinkle with mirin and lime juice and steam just until opaque. Do not overcook or the prawns/shrimp will be tough. Serve with lime halves for squeezing.

Vietnamese summer rolls

These fresh spring rolls are a far cry from the deep fried Chinese version we are most familiar with. Clean, cool and completely delicious, they are perfect for a summer's day.

25 g/1 oz. fine rice vermicelli

6 rice-paper discs or wrappers (available in oriental stores)

200 g/7 oz. cooked prawns/shrimp, halved lengthways if large

a bunch of fresh mint, stalks removed

a bunch of fresh coriander/cilantro or Thai basil, stalks removed

2 carrots, grated

30 g/½ cup beansprouts

hoi sin dipping sauce, to serve

Makes 6

Break up the rice vermicelli into smaller lengths, about 8–10 cm/3–4 inches, and cook according to the package instructions. Refresh the noodles under cold water, then leave to drain.

Now get ready to roll. It's best to do this with an assembly line: start with a large shallow dish of warm water to soak the rice-paper discs in; next, you will need a plate covered with a clean tea/dish towel, on which to drape them once soaked; then the prawns/shrimp, herb leaves, vermicelli and other fresh ingredients, each in a separate bowl.

Soak a rice-paper disc in the warm water for 15 seconds until translucent and pliable, then move to the plate. Start to make a pile of the ingredients in the middle of the disc. Start with 2 whole mint leaves, placed shiny side down, then the noodles, grated carrot and beansprouts, then 2–3 prawns/shrimp, and finally a good handful of coriander/cilantro (the trick to a good summer roll is not being shy with your herbs).

Roll up tightly from the bottom, fold in the sides, then finish rolling up the cylinder. Repeat the process for each roll, topping up the warm water when necessary. It is best to make each roll individually as the rice-paper discs tend to be quite sticky. Serve accompanied by the hoi sin dipping sauce.

125 g/4 oz. crab meat

50 g/2 oz. cooked and shelled prawns/shrimp, chopped

4 canned water chestnuts, finely chopped

2 spring onions/scallions, finely chopped

a 2.5-cm/1-inch piece of fresh ginger, peeled and grated

1 small chilli, deseeded and finely chopped

1 tablespoon fresh coriander/cilantro, chopped

1 tablespoon light soy sauce

20 x 8–9 cm/3½ inch round wonton wrappers

toasted sesame seeds, to sprinkle

Soy and Ginger Sauce (see page 19), to serve

a steamer

Serves 4–6

These bite-size morsels are typical of Chinese dim sum – they look elegant, smell tantalizing and taste good! Use fresh crab meat for the very best flavour. If you do need to use frozen crab meat, make sure it is well drained before using.

crab wonton wraps

In a bowl mix together the crab meat, prawns/shrimp, water chestnuts, spring onions/scallions, ginger, chilli, coriander/cilantro and soy sauce.

Brush the edges of a wonton wrapper with water. Place a heaped teaspoon of filling in the centre. Draw up the edges and press together. Repeat to make 20 wonton wraps. Cover until ready to cook.

In a small bowl, combine the dipping sauce ingredients.

Put a layer of silicone paper in the base of a steamer and arrange the wonton wraps in the steamer, making sure they do not touch each other. Place over a pan of boiling water, cover and steam for 5 minutes. Cook in batches if necessary.

Sprinkle with toasted sesame seeds and serve with the Soy and Ginger Sauce.

Vietnamese spiced squid

25 g/1 oz. cellophane rice noodles (rice vermicelli), about 1 small bundle

90 ml/½ cup peanut oil

3 spring onions/scallions, chopped

a 3-cm/1-inch piece of fresh ginger, peeled and grated

2 garlic cloves, chopped

16 prepared, cleaned baby squid with tentacles reserved*

325 g/12 oz. minced/ground pork

2–3 'petals' of 1 star anise, finely crushed (about ¼ teaspoon ground)

¼ teaspoon cracked black pepper

1 tablespoon Thai or Vietnamese fish sauce

a pinch of sugar

a pinch of sea salt

a handful of mixed Asian herbs, to serve

Nuóc Cham dipping sauce (see page 19), to serve

Makes 16

This appetizing dish of stuffed baby squid, spiced with star anise, ginger and pepper, is a fine example of Vietnamese cuisine. Nuóc cham is the traditional Vietnamese dipping sauce, but you could use soy sauce or chilli sauce.

To prepare the stuffing, pour boiling water over the noodles and let soak for 4 minutes or according to the instructions on the packet. Drain well, coarsely chop the noodles and transfer to a large bowl.

Put 1 tablespoon of the peanut oil into a wok, heat well, swirl to coat, then add the spring onions/scallions, ginger and garlic. Stir-fry for a few minutes until softened, then add to the bowl. Chop the squid tentacles and add to the ingredients in the bowl. Add the pork, star anise, pepper, fish sauce, sugar and salt and mix.

Stuff the squid bodies, leaving a little space at the top. Secure closed with toothpicks.

Heat the remaining oil in a frying pan/skillet and add the squid. Cook gently for 10–12 minutes, until lightly browned in places and cooked through.

Slice the squid or leave them whole, then serve with fresh herbs and nuóc cham or other South-east Asian dipping sauces.

*Note To prepare the squid, cut off the tentacles and chop them coarsely. Cut off and discard the eye sections. Rinse out the bodies, discarding the tiny transparent quill. If you can't find squid with tentacles, buy an extra body, chop it coarsely, then add to the stuffing mixture.

Thai fish cakes

500 g/1 lb. white fish fillets, such as cod, haddock or monkfish

2 tablespoons Red Curry Paste (page 10)

2 tablespoons Thai fish sauce

60 g/¾ cup thin green beans or Chinese longbeans, very finely sliced

5 kaffir lime leaves, finely chopped

peanut or sunflower oil, for frying

Cucumber relish

250 ml/1 cup rice vinegar

2 tablespoons sugar

a 5-cm/2-inch piece of cucumber (unpeeled), coarsely chopped

1 small carrot, chopped

3 pink Thai shallots, finely sliced

1 medium fresh red chilli, finely sliced

1 tablespoon crushed roasted peanuts (optional)

an electric deep-fryer (optional)

Makes 20 cakes

Everywhere in Thailand, fish cakes are a favourite traditional dish. While they are simple to make, they are an excellent benchmark of the good Thai cook. With a bit of practice, you will be able to create a cake of just the right texture and consistency of ingredients.

To make the relish, put the vinegar and sugar in a saucepan and heat, stirring until the sugar dissolves. Boil to produce a thin syrup. Remove from the heat and let cool.

When the syrup is cool, add the cucumber, carrot, shallots, chilli and peanuts, if using. Mix thoroughly and set aside.

To mince the fish, cut the fillets into pieces and put in a food processor or blender. Pulse to form a smooth paste, then transfer to a large bowl.

Put the curry paste in the bowl and, using your fingers, blend thoroughly with the minced fish. Add the fish sauce, green beans and kaffir lime leaves and knead together. Shape into small flat cakes about 5 cm/2 inches across and 1.25 cm/½ inch thick.

Fill a wok or deep-fryer one-third full with the oil or to the manufacturer's recommended level. Heat until a scrap of noodle will puff up immediately.

Working in batches if necessary, add the fish cakes and fry until golden on both sides. Remove with a slotted spoon and drain on paper towels. Serve the fish cakes with the cucumber relish.

chicken wings with lemongrass and sweet and hot sauce

3 stalks of lemongrass, finely chopped

2 small chillies, finely chopped

3 tablespoons oyster sauce

1 tablespoon Thai fish sauce

1 teaspoon sugar

500 g/1 lb. chicken winglets (also known as drumettes)

peanut or sunflower oil, for deep-frying

To serve

Sweet and Hot Sauce (see page 29)

sprigs of coriander/cilantro

an electric deep-fryer (optional)

Serves 4

For this dish only the thick part of the wings (little drumsticks) are used, marinated in a blend of lemongrass and chilli. The crunchiness of the deep-fried lemongrass on the little drumsticks makes for an interesting texture.

Put the lemongrass, chillies, oyster sauce, fish sauce and sugar in a bowl and beat with a fork. Add the chicken winglets, turn to coat and set aside to marinate for 15 minutes.

Fill a wok or deep-fryer one-third full with the oil or to the manufacturer's recommended level. Heat until a scrap of noodle will puff up immediately.

Working in batches if necessary, fry the chicken wings until golden brown. Remove with a slotted spoon, drain and serve with sweet and hot sauce and sprigs of coriander/cilantro.

Note If you are unable to find chicken winglets, buy the whole wings and cut off the last 2 joints. Use them for another recipe or to make stock.

Chicken satays are popular throughout Southeast Asia but in Vietnam, Cambodia and China, duck satays are common too. Duck is often served in the Chinese tradition of sweet and sour with a fruity sauce. You can buy ready-made bottled plum sauce in Chinese markets and most supermarkets.

duck satay with grilled pineapple and plum sauce

700 g/1 lb. 9 oz. duck breasts or boned thighs, sliced into thin, bite-size strips

1–2 tablespoons peanut or coconut oil, for brushing

1 small pineapple, peeled, cored and sliced

Chinese plum sauce, to serve

Marinade

2–3 tablespoons light soy sauce

freshly squeezed juice of 1 lime

1–2 teaspoons sugar

1–2 garlic cloves, crushed

25 g/1 oz. fresh ginger, peeled and grated

1 small onion, grated

1–2 teaspoons ground coriander

1 teaspoon salt

a packet of wooden or bamboo skewers, soaked in water before use

Serves 4

To make the marinade, put the soy sauce and lime juice in a bowl with the sugar and mix until it dissolves. Add the garlic, ginger and grated onion and stir in the coriander and salt.

Place the strips of duck in a bowl and pour over the marinade. Toss well, cover and chill in the refrigerator for at least 4 hours. Thread the duck strips onto the skewers and brush them with oil.

Prepare a charcoal or conventional grill/broiler. Cook the satays for 3–4 minutes on each side, until the duck is nicely browned. Grill/broil the slices of pineapple at the same time. When browned, cut them into bite-size pieces and serve with the duck. Drizzle with the plum sauce to serve.

This dish makes excellent finger food for parties and often appears on Thai restaurant menus as a starter. It can be served on its own or alternatively with a hot sauce to add a more spicy flavour.

pork toasts

6 slices of white bread, crusts trimmed and each slice cut into 4

4 small garlic cloves, finely chopped

3 coriander/cilantro roots, chopped

250 g/8 oz. minced/ground pork

1 egg

2 tablespoons Thai fish sauce

a pinch of freshly ground white pepper

peanut or sunflower/safflower oil, for deep-frying

To serve

coriander/cilantro leaves

a 5-cm/2-inch piece of cucumber, quartered lengthways, then thinly sliced crossways

1 fresh red chilli, finely sliced into rings

a baking sheet

an electric deep-fryer (optional)

Serves 4

Preheat the oven to 120°C (250°F) Gas ½. Arrange the pieces of bread on a baking sheet, put in the oven for 5 minutes, then remove.

Using a mortar and pestle or blender, either pound or grind the garlic and coriander/cilantro roots together. Put in a bowl, then add the pork, egg, fish sauce and white pepper and mix thoroughly. Put 1 teaspoon of the mixture on each piece of toast.

Fill a wok or deep-fryer one-third full with the oil or to the manufacturer's recommended level. Heat until a scrap of noodle will puff up immediately.

Working in batches of 2–3 at a time, fry the toasts for 2–3 minutes until browned. Remove with a slotted spoon, drain on paper towels, arrange on a large plate and serve with the coriander/cilantro leaves, cucumber and chilli.

steamed pork buns

1 tablespoon peanut oil

1 tablespoon chopped onion

1 garlic clove, crushed

125 g/4 oz. Chinese barbecued/grilled pork, finely chopped*

2 spring onions/scallions, chopped

1 teaspoon soy sauce

freshly ground black pepper

½ teaspoon sugar

¼ teaspoon sesame oil

Bun dough

350 g/2½ cups plain/all-purpose flour

2½ teaspoons baking powder

1 tablespoon sugar

½ teaspoon salt

1 tablespoon peanut oil

¼ teaspoon sesame oil

8 pieces of greaseproof/wax paper, 10 cm/4 inches square

Makes 8

If you live near a Chinatown market, you can buy their delicious grilled pork. If you don't, try the home-style version, below, reserving a little for the buns.

Heat the oil in a wok, add the onion and garlic and stir-fry until golden. Add the pork, spring onions/scallions, soy sauce, pepper, sugar and sesame oil, stir-fry quickly at high heat, then reduce the heat and simmer gently for about 5 minutes. Let cool.

To make the dough, sift the flour and baking powder into a bowl, then stir in the sugar and salt. Stir in the peanut and sesame oils and knead to form a soft dough. Cover and set aside for 1 hour.

Turn out the dough onto a work surface and knead for 5 minutes. Divide into 8, then roll each piece into a ball and flatten to a disc. Put one-eighth of the filling in the middle of each disc, then gradually work the outside edge of the disc around and over the top to enclose the filling. Seal.

Put 8 pieces of greaseproof/wax paper into one or more tiers of a steamer. Brush the paper with oil. Put the buns, sealed side down and well apart, onto the pieces of paper. Steam over simmering water for about 30 minutes, until well puffed, then serve.

*Chinese Barbecued/Grilled Pork Cut 1 kg/2 lb. pork tenderloin into two long strips lengthwise. Rub with 1 tablespoon black pepper and 1 tablespoon Chinese five-spice powder. Put 4 tablespoons soy sauce into a shallow dish and stir in 2 teaspoons sesame oil. Add the pork and turn to coat well. Cover and chill overnight. Next day, let return to room temperature for 1 hour, then cook on a barbecue/outdoor grill or roast on a rack in a preheated oven at 200°C (400°F) Gas 6 for about 15 minutes. Reduce the heat to 175°C (350°F) Gas 4 and continue roasting for about 20 minutes. Let rest for 20 minutes before cutting.

2 teaspoons peanut or sesame oil

4 shallots, finely chopped

2 garlic cloves, finely chopped

450 g/1 lb. minced/ground pork

2 tablespoons Thai fish sauce

2 teaspoons five-spice powder

2 teaspoons sugar

2 handfuls of fresh white or brown breadcrumbs

sea salt and freshly ground black pepper

Sweet and sour sauce

2 teaspoons peanut oil

1 garlic clove, finely chopped

1 fresh red chilli, deseeded and finely chopped

2 tablespoons roasted peanuts, finely chopped

1 tablespoon Thai fish sauce

2 tablespoons rice wine vinegar

2 tablespoons hoisin sauce

4 tablespoons coconut milk

1–2 teaspoons sugar, to taste

a pinch of sea salt

a packet of short wooden or bamboo skewers, soaked in water before use

Serves 4

pork kofta kebabs with sweet and sour sauce

These Asian-style meatball kebabs are best served with a hot, spicy dipping sauce and noodles. The sweet hoisin sauce is available in larger supermarkets and Asian markets.

To make the sauce, heat the oil in a small wok or heavy-based frying pan/skillet. Stir in the garlic and chilli and, when they begin to colour, add the peanuts. Stir for a few minutes until the natural oil from the peanuts begins to weep. Add all the remaining ingredients (except the sugar and salt) along with 100 ml/½ cup water. Let the mixture bubble up for 1 minute. Adjust the sweetness and seasoning to taste with sugar and some salt and set aside.

To make the meatballs, heat the oil in a wok or a heavy-based frying pan/skillet. Add the shallots and garlic – when they begin to brown, turn off the heat and leave to cool. Put the minced/ground pork into a bowl, tip in the stir-fried shallot and garlic, fish sauce, five-spice powder and sugar and season with a little salt and lots of pepper. Using your hands, knead the mixture so it is well combined. Cover and chill in the refrigerator for 2–3 hours. Knead the mixture again then tip in the breadcrumbs. Knead well to bind. Divide the mixture into roughly 20 portions and roll into balls. Thread them onto the prepared skewers. Prepare a charcoal or conventional grill or heat the broiler. Cook the kebabs for 3–4 minutes on each side, turning them from time to time, until browned.

Reheat the sauce. Serve the kofta with noodles and the hot sweet and sour sauce on the side for dipping.

500 g/1 lb. beef sirloin, sliced against the grain into bite-size pieces

1 tablespoon peanut oil

Peanut sauce

60 ml/¼ cup peanut or vegetable oil

4–5 garlic cloves, crushed

4–5 dried serrano chillies, deseeded and ground with a pestle and mortar

1–2 teaspoons curry powder

60 g/½ cup roasted peanuts, finely ground

To serve

a small bunch of fresh coriander/cilantro

a small bunch of fresh mint

lime wedges

a packet of short wooden or bamboo skewers, soaked in water before use

Serves 4–6

fiery beef satay in peanut sauce

Beef, pork or chicken satays cooked in, or served with, a fiery peanut sauce are hugely popular throughout Southeast Asia. This particular sauce is a great favourite in Thailand, Vietnam and Indonesia. It is best to make your own but commercial brands are available under the banner satay or sate sauce.

To make the sauce, heat the oil in a heavy-based saucepan and stir in the garlic until it begins to colour. Add the chillies, curry powder and the peanuts and stir over a gentle heat, until the mixture forms a paste. Remove from the heat and leave to cool.

Put the beef pieces in a bowl. Beat the peanut oil into the sauce and tip the mixture onto the beef. Mix well, so that the beef is evenly coated and thread the meat onto the prepared skewers.

Prepare a charcoal or conventional grill or heat the broiler. Cook the satays for 2–3 minutes on each side, then serve the skewered meat with the fresh herbs to wrap around each tasty morsel.

spicy beef and coconut kofta kebabs

1 teaspoon coriander seeds

1 teaspoon cumin seeds

175 g/1⅓ cups desiccated or freshly grated coconut

1 tablespoon coconut oil

4 shallots, peeled and finely chopped

2 garlic cloves, finely chopped

1–2 fresh red chillies, deseeded and finely chopped

350 g/12 oz. lean minced/ground beef

1 beaten egg, to bind

sea salt and freshly ground black pepper

To serve

2–3 tablespoons freshly grated or desiccated coconut

lime wedges

a packet of short wooden or bamboo skewers, soaked in water before use

Serves 4

Variations of this Asian dish can be found at street stalls from Sri Lanka to the Philippines and South Africa to the West Indies. Simple and tasty, the kofta are delicious served with wedges of fresh lime or a dipping sauce of your choice.

In a small heavy-based frying pan/skillet, dry roast the coriander and cumin seeds until they give off a nutty aroma. Using a mortar and pestle, or a spice grinder, grind the roasted seeds to a powder.

In the same pan, dry roast the coconut until it begins to colour and give off a nutty aroma. Tip it onto a plate to cool.

Heat the coconut oil in the same small heavy-based pan and stir in the shallots, garlic and chillies, until fragrant and beginning to colour. Tip them onto a plate to cool.

Put the minced/ground beef in a bowl and add the ground spices, toasted coconut and shallot mixture. Season with salt and pepper and use a fork to mix all the ingredients together, adding a little egg to bind it (you may not need it all). Knead the mixture with your hands and mould it into little balls. Thread the balls onto the prepared skewers.

Prepare a charcoal or conventional grill or heat the broiler. Cook the kebabs for 2–3 minutes on each side. Sprinkle the cooked kofta with the toasted coconut and serve with the wedges of lime to squeeze over them.

1 large sirloin steak, 3–4 cm/
1–1½ inches thick, about 500 g/
1 lb., trimmed of fat

Marinade

2 tablespoons tamari or other soy
sauce

1 teaspoon toasted sesame oil

1–2 teaspoons sugar

1 garlic clove, crushed

a 3-cm/1-inch piece of fresh
ginger, peeled and finely grated

2 spring onions/scallions, trimmed
and chopped

1–2 bird's eye chillies, red or
green, deseeded and chopped

a pinch of salt

White radish kimchi

1 teaspoon sugar

2 tablespoons rice vinegar

1 large garlic clove, crushed

a pinch of sea salt

250 g/8 oz. daikon (white radish),
peeled and grated

lettuce leaves, to serve

Serves 4

Bulgogi is a Korean delight – as popular with tourists as it is with the locals. Ginger and toasted sesame oil are included in the marinade, while chillies make their inevitable appearance, though the amount is up to you. Bulgogi is an appetizer that can be made and served in two ways. Always sliced very thinly, the beef strips can be wide or narrow. The wide ones are served with rice and condiments, while the narrow ones are rolled up in lettuce leaves – an entirely satisfying way of eating this dish.

bulgogi

Make the kimchi 1–3 days before using. Put the sugar, vinegar, garlic and salt into a bowl. Put the grated radish into a dish towel and squeeze well to remove excess water. Add the radish to the bowl and mix until well coated. While the jar is still hot, pour the kimchi into the jar and seal tightly. Let cool then refrigerate until ready to use.

Freeze the steak for 1 hour so it will be easy to slice very thinly. Remove the steak from the freezer, then slice thinly crossways.

To make the marinade, put the tamari or soy, sesame oil and sugar into a bowl and whisk well. Stir in the garlic, ginger, spring onions/scallions, chillies and salt, then add the beef strips, mix well to coat, cover and refrigerate for several hours to develop the flavours.

Heat a stove-top grill pan or frying pan/skillet until very hot. Sear the strips of steak briefly on both sides until just done, working in batches so you don't overcrowd the pan. Either pile onto a serving plate or divide between 4 plates and serve with lettuce and kimchi.

A quick source of sustenance or a satisfying meal, this collection of warming, hearty soups and broths features both classic and contemporary recipes. Singing with spice and bursting with flavour there's a recipe to suit every palate.

soups

vegetables with miso and sake

1 tablespoon vegetable oil

2 garlic cloves, crushed

200 g/6½ oz. sugar snap peas

200 g/6½ oz. baby courgettes/zucchini, chopped into chunks on the diagonal

200 g/6½ oz. frozen edamame beans, defrosted

shoyu or tamari soy sauce, to taste (optional)

Sauce

2 heaped teaspoons red or brown miso paste

1 tablespoon mirin (Japanese rice wine)

1 tablespoon sake

150 ml dashi/⅔ cup or vegetable stock

1 tablespoon cornflour/cornstarch

Serves 4

A dash of miso adds depth to this simple soup. You'll find edamame beans, also called soya beans, in the freezer section of the supermarket.

Combine all the sauce ingredients in a bowl and set aside.

Heat the oil in a wok or large frying pan/skillet until hot, then add the garlic and stir-fry over high heat for 30 seconds. Throw in the sugar snap peas and courgettes/zucchini and stir-fry for 2–3 minutes. Add the edamame beans and toss well, then pour in the sauce. Bring to the boil, then reduce the heat and simmer, stirring occasionally, for about 3 minutes, or until the vegetables are cooked through but still crunchy.

Taste and add a dash of soy sauce if you think it needs it. Divide between 4 bowls and serve immediately.

2 tablespoons dried wakame seaweed

3 tablespoons miso paste

125 g/4 oz. firm tofu, cut into 1-cm/½-inch cubes

1 spring onion/scallion, trimmed and finely sliced

Shichimi Togarashi (see page 13) or ground sansho pepper, to serve

Dashi*

1 piece dried kombu seaweed, 5 cm/2 inches square

6 tablespoons dried bonito flakes (ana-katsuo)

Serves 4

Instant dashi powder is widely available in larger supermarkets and Japanese stores. Labelled 'dashi-no-moto', it is freeze-dried and very convenient. Use 1–2 teaspoons for this recipe.

Classic in its simplicity, miso soup warms and entices at the beginning of a Japanese meal. The soup is definitely worth making – serve it as the Japanese do, in beautiful lacquer bowls.

miso and wakame soup with Japanese seven-spice

To make the dashi, put the kombu into a large saucepan and add 550 ml/2½ cups water. Bring to the boil and immediately remove the kombu (don't let it boil or it will become bitter).

Add the bonito flakes to the boiling water, simmer gently for 2–3 minutes, then remove from the heat. Let stand for a few minutes until the bonito settles to the bottom of the pan. Strain through a sieve/strainer lined with muslin/cheesecloth and reserve the liquid. (Alternatively, add 1–2 teaspoons instant dashi powder to the boiling water and stir to dissolve.)

Meanwhile, soak the wakame in a large bowl of water for 10–15 minutes until fully opened. Drain and cut into small pieces.

Put the miso into a cup or bowl and mix with a few spoonfuls of dashi. Return the dashi to a low heat and add the diluted miso. Add the wakame and tofu to the pan and turn up the heat. Just before it reaches boiling point, add the finely chopped spring onion/scallion and immediately remove from the heat. Do not boil.

Serve hot in individual soup bowls with a little shichimi togarashi or ground sansho pepper for sprinkling.

cauliflower, mushroom and coconut soup

While cauliflower is familiar as an ingredient in stir-fry recipes, prized for its crunchiness, here it is cooked with mushrooms and coconut milk, so the cauliflower absorbs the flavour of coconut, making it light and sweet.

600 ml/2¾ cups coconut cream

2 stalks of lemongrass, finely sliced

a 5-cm/2-inch piece of fresh galangal or ginger, peeled and finely sliced into rings

4 kaffir lime leaves, coarsely torn into quarters

1 small cauliflower, cut into florets

125 g/2½ cups small button mushrooms, cut into halves or quarters, according to size

3 tablespoons light soy sauce

1 teaspoon sugar

600 ml/2¾ cups vegetable stock

4 fresh small red or green chillies, slightly crushed

3 tablespoons lemon or lime juice

coriander/cilantro leaves, to serve

Serves 4

Put the coconut cream, lemongrass, galangal, kaffir lime leaves, cauliflower, mushrooms, soy sauce, sugar and stock in a large saucepan and bring to the boil. Reduce the heat and simmer until the cauliflower is al dente (cooked, but still firm). Remove from the heat and add the chillies and lemon juice. Stir once, pour into a serving bowl and top with coriander/cilantro leaves.

450 g/1 lb. large uncooked prawns/shrimp

1 tablespoon sunflower or groundnut oil

1 teaspoon grated lime zest

1.25 litres/5½ cups fish or chicken stock

2 lemongrass stalks, thinly sliced

3 garlic cloves, halved

a 2.5-cm/1-inch piece of fresh ginger, unpeeled and sliced

a small bunch of fresh coriander/cilantro, chopped, stalks reserved

3 fresh or dried kaffir lime leaves

a bunch of spring onions/scallions, thinly sliced, green and white parts separated

2–3 red chillies, halved and deseeded

1 large carrot, cut into matchstick strips

2–3 tablespoons Thai fish sauce

freshly squeezed juice of up to 2 limes

1–2 pinches of sugar

180 g/6 oz. Asian greens, such as pak choi/bok choy or mustard greens, sliced

sea salt and freshly ground black pepper

lime wedges, to serve

Serves 4

It's the lime juice and kaffir lime leaves that make this hot and sour soup so addictively delicious. The lime cuts through the heat of the chilli and counterbalances the salty piquancy of the other essential ingredient – Thai fish sauce or nam pla.

hot and sour soup with prawns

Shell and devein the prawns/shrimp, then toss 8–12 of them in the oil and lime zest and season with a little salt. Roughly chop the remainder into 3–4 pieces each. Keep all the prawns/shrimp chilled while you make the soup.

Put the stock, lemongrass, garlic, ginger, coriander/cilantro stalks, kaffir lime leaves, the green parts of the onions and 1–2 chillies in a saucepan, bring to the boil and simmer, covered, for 15–20 minutes. Strain and return to the pan.

Add the carrot and cook for 3–4 minutes, then add the white part of the onion/scallion and the chopped prawns/shrimp. Simmer for a few minutes, then add fish sauce and lime juice to taste. Adjust the seasoning with salt, pepper and a pinch or two of sugar. The soup should be fairly piquant and sharp.

Meanwhile, heat a ridged stove-top grill pan or frying pan/skillet until hot, add the reserved whole prawns/shrimp and quickly fry them for 2–3 minutes until they turn pink and opaque.

Reheat the soup if necessary and stir in the Asian greens and most of the coriander/cilantro leaves, then ladle the hot soup into bowls and add 2–3 whole prawns/shrimp to each bowl. Garnish with the remaining coriander/cilantro leaves and remaining chilli, shredded, then serve with lime wedges.

Chicken stock (optional)

1 chicken carcass

1 celery stick

1 carrot

1 sprig fresh thyme

1 onion, halved

a few fresh parsley stalks

a few black peppercorns

Soup

1 litre/4 cups chicken stock

5 kaffir lime leaves

fresh juice of 2 limes

2 lemongrass sticks, bruised

a 5-cm/2-inch piece of galangal, thinly sliced (or a smaller amount of fresh ginger)

3 tablespoons nam pla fish sauce

250 ml/1 cup coconut milk

15 prawns/shrimp

3 red chillies, deseeded and chopped

handful of fresh coriander/cilantro leaves

Serves 6

Thai coconut and lemongrass soup with prawns

The flavours here vary from deep and complex to clean and fresh all at the same time and would fool anyone into thinking you had spent hours slaving over it. It is a great soup when you are slightly under the weather – the coconut milk soothes while the chilli and galangal blast away any potential viruses.

To make the chicken stock, put all the ingredients and 2.5 litres/10 cups cold water in a large saucepan and bring to the boil. Reduce the heat and simmer for at least 3 hours. Skim off any fat from the surface and strain off the liquid. If you are stuck for time, you can buy good-quality free-range, organic chicken stock in good supermarkets.

To make the soup, put the chicken stock, lime leaves, lime juice, lemongrass, galangal and fish sauce in a large pan and bring to the boil. Add the coconut milk, prawns/shrimp and chillies (reserving a little for serving) and continue to cook for a couple of minutes until the prawns/shrimp are cooked through. Add the majority of the coriander/cilantro leaves, then check the seasoning and add more fish sauce if necessary. Serve in bowls with the reserved chillies and remaining coriander/cilantro scattered on top.

Shiitake mushrooms have a unique, earthy savouriness that few other non-meaty ingredients have and which the Japanese call umami. This means they can make a light broth very flavoursome. Soba noodles are made from buckwheat and go well with the delicate salmon.

salmon, soba noodle and shiitake broth

1 tablespoon groundnut oil

250 g/8 oz. shiitake mushrooms, washed, dried and halved

a 3-cm/1¼-inch piece of fresh ginger, unpeeled and sliced

three 8-g/¼-inch sachets miso stock powder

1.5 litres/3 quarts boiling water

200 g/6½ oz. buckwheat soba noodles

2 tablespoons light soy sauce

4 tablespoons sake (rice wine)

2 tablespoons granulated sugar

four 125-g/4-oz. salmon fillets, cut into chunks

6 spring onions/scallions, sliced

a pinch of chilli powder

sesame oil, to drizzle

Serves 4

Heat the oil in a large saucepan over medium heat and add the mushrooms and ginger. Cook gently for 5 minutes, or until softened.

Put the miso stock powder and boiling water in a jug/pitcher and stir until dissolved. Pour into the pan with the mushrooms. Bring to the boil and simmer for 5 minutes to allow the flavours to infuse. Add the noodles and bring to the boil, then cook for a further 4 minutes, or until just tender (they will continue to cook while you dish up so don't overdo them). Add the soy sauce, sake and sugar to the broth and gently lower in the salmon. Reduce the heat to low so the broth is only just boiling and poach the salmon for 3–4 minutes, or until cooked through.

Fish out the noodles and transfer to bowls. Using a slotted spoon, lift out the salmon and place on top of the noodles. Ladle the remaining soup into the bowls, scatter with the spring onions/scallions and chilli powder and drizzle with sesame oil.

2 tablespoons peanut or sunflower oil

2 garlic cloves, coarsely chopped

1.25 litres/5 cups chicken stock

400 g/3 cups cooked rice (from about 150 g/1 cup raw rice)

500 g/1 lb. skinless boneless chicken breasts or thighs, thinly sliced

1 teaspoon chopped preserved vegetables (tang chi)

2 tablespoons Thai fish sauce

2 tablespoons soy sauce

1 teaspoon sugar

a 2.5-cm/1-inch piece of fresh ginger, peeled and cut into fine shreds

½ teaspoon freshly ground white pepper

To serve

1 spring onion/scallion, finely sliced

a few fresh coriander/cilantro leaves

Serves 4

This is a staple dish in the Thai diet. Rice soup is to the Thai breakfast menu what cereals are in the West. Then, at the other end of the day, it continues to provide a quick source of sustenance, when late night revellers stop for a middle-of-the-night bowl of rice soup at any of the 24-hour food stalls you find in Thai cities.

chicken rice soup

Heat the oil in a small frying pan/skillet add the garlic and fry until golden brown. Set aside to infuse, reserving both the oil and the garlic.

Heat the stock in a large saucepan, add the cooked rice and slices of chicken and bring to the boil.

Stir in the preserved vegetables, fish sauce, soy sauce, sugar, ginger and white pepper and simmer gently for about 30 seconds, or until the chicken is cooked through.

Transfer to a serving bowl and trickle over a little of the reserved garlic oil. Top with finely sliced spring onion/scallion and fresh coriander/cilantro leaves.

Sparerib and Tamarind Soup, or Tom Som, is a favourite inside Thailand. The sparerib-based stock includes a mixture of garlic, shallots, ginger and tamarind water – the latter contributing its strong, sour taste. It offers an exciting alternative to the traditional Tom Yam soup.

sparerib and tamarind soup

1 teaspoon black peppercorns

1 tablespoon finely chopped coriander/cilantro root

2 garlic cloves

4 pink Thai shallots or 2 regular ones

1 tablespoon peanut or sunflower oil

1.25 litres/5 cups chicken stock

500 g/1 lb. small pork spareribs, chopped into 2.5-cm/1-inch pieces

a 5-cm/2-inch piece of fresh ginger, finely sliced into matchsticks

2 tablespoons tamarind water

2 tablespoons sugar

3 tablespoons Thai fish sauce

4 spring onions/scallions, chopped into 2.5-cm/1-inch lengths

Serves 4

Using a mortar and pestle, pound the peppercorns, coriander/cilantro root, garlic and shallots to form a paste.

Heat the oil in a large saucepan, add the paste and fry for 5 seconds, stirring well. Add the stock and bring to the boil, stirring well. Add the spareribs and return to the boil.

Add the ginger, tamarind water, sugar, fish sauce and spring onions/scallions. Return to the boil again and simmer for 1 minute. Ladle into a bowl and serve.

Note: Preparing tamarind
If you can't find tamarind water, or the pulp in block form, tamarind paste is available in small bottles in Oriental supermarkets. For this recipe, mix 1 tablespoon paste with 1 tablespoon water.

Tamarind pulp is also available in block form. To prepare your own tamarind water, mix 1 tablespoon tamarind pulp in a bowl with 150 ml/2/3 cup hot water, mashing with a fork. As you mix the pulp and water, the water absorbs the taste of the tamarind. When the water is cool, you can squeeze the tamarind pulp to extract more juice (and you can remove any seeds). Pour off the juice into a container and set aside for use in recipes. It will keep for about a week in the refrigerator.

750 g/1½ oz. trimmed braising beef, cut into small chunks

7 white peppercorns

a 3-cm/1-inch piece of fresh galangal, peeled and sliced, or fresh ginger

1 teaspoon freshly grated nutmeg

¼ teaspoon ground turmeric

325 ml/14 oz. coconut milk

sea salt

Spice paste

2–3 tablespoons peanut oil

1 teaspoon ground coriander

7 white peppercorns

4 red bird's eye chillies

2 teaspoons brown sugar

1 garlic clove, chopped

5 fresh Thai basil (or sweet basil) leaves

a large handful of fresh coriander/cilantro, about 25 g/ 1 oz., coarsely chopped

8 pink Thai shallots or 1 regular shallot

a few cardamom seeds (not pods)

a 2-cm/1-inch piece of fresh ginger, peeled and chopped

a small piece of shrimp paste, toasted in a dry frying pan/skillet or the oven, or 1 teaspoon anchovy paste mixed with 1 tablespoon fish sauce

Serves 4–6

Indonesian beef and coconut soup

This strongly spiced and flavoured soup has slices of meat swimming in plenty of creamy broth. It is quintessentially Indonesian in its spicing, influenced by the nation's diverse population and topography. Wave after wave of settlers entered Indonesia long ago, from Malays, Indians and Chinese to Arab traders. Living on the world's largest archipelago and comprising around 350 ethnic groups, Indonesians are a varied people and so is their cuisine. What comes across in dishes like this soup is a fascinating mixture of spices and flavours.

Put all the spice paste ingredients into a blender or a food processor and grind to a thick paste, adding a dash of water to keep the blades turning if necessary. Set aside.

Put the beef, peppercorns, galangal, nutmeg, turmeric and salt into a saucepan, add 1.5 litres/1½ quarts water and bring to a boil, skimming off the foam as it rises to the surface. Stir, reduce the heat and simmer uncovered for about 1½ hours, until the meat is mostly tender and the stock is well reduced.

Strain the beef, discarding the galangal slices and peppercorns, but reserving the beef and stock. Return the stock to the pan, then stir in the spice paste. Bring to a boil, reduce the heat, add the beef and simmer for 5 minutes, stirring regularly.

Finally, add the coconut milk and simmer gently for a few minutes. Serve the soup on its own or with a small mound of plain rice.

4 tablespoons toasted cashews

Broth base

1 lemongrass stick

700 ml/3 cups cold beef stock

2 tablespoons soy sauce

2 tablespoons nam pla fish sauce

2 tablespoons palm sugar

grated zest and juice of 1 lime

400-ml/14-oz. can coconut milk

Soup

200 g/7 oz. thin rice noodles

2 teaspoons toasted sesame oil,
plus extra to drizzle

2 eggs, lightly beaten

2 garlic cloves, crushed

a 5-cm/2-inch piece of fresh
galangal or ginger, grated

2 small red chillies, deseeded and
thinly sliced, plus extra to garnish

2 kaffir lime leaves

2 big handfuls of spinach leaves

4 chestnut mushrooms, sliced

2 tablespoons chopped fresh
coriander/cilantro, plus extra
leaves to garnish

5 tablespoons julienned carrot

4 Baby Gem lettuce leaves, sliced

1 shallot, julienned

40 g/½ cup beansprouts

280 g/10 oz. sirloin steak, sliced
as thinly as you can

Serves 2

Thai beef noodle soup

Mai Fun noodles are a good choice here but, if they are not available at your nearest Asian store, there will definitely be a rice noodle substitute available that will work in this recipe.

To make the broth base, bash the lemongrass carefully with the handle of a knife to bruise it. Place it with all the other broth base ingredients in a saucepan, bring to a simmer and taste. Add more seasoning if required and discard the lemongrass.

Blanch the noodles in a pan of boiling water for 5 minutes or until cooked, and refresh under cold water.

Put the toasted sesame oil in a non-stick frying pan/skillet and heat. Pour the beaten eggs into the hot pan and fry gently, allowing no colour to develop and without stirring. You will eventually get a sort of egg pancake. Let cool slightly to handle, then transfer it to a board and slice it into 3-mm/⅛-inch strips. Divide the pieces of egg between 2 bowls.

Divide all the remaining ingredients that make up the soup between the bowls, along with the blanched noodles. Bring the broth base back to a simmer, then pour it into the soup bowls – the hot broth will reheat and/or cook all the ingredients. Garnish each bowl with whole coriander/cilantro leaves, a few slices of chilli, a drizzle of sesame oil and the toasted cashew nuts.

From the ubiquitous chicken Pad Thai to delicious Japchae from Korea, noodles and rice are the mainstay of Asian cuisine. Simple to prepare, these dishes are perfect for a weekday meal.

noodles and rice

noodles with gomadare sesame seed sauce

200 g/6½ oz. buckwheat soba noodles

Gomadare sauce

2 tablespoons mirin (sweetened rice wine)

1 tablespoon sesame seeds, lightly toasted

2 tablespoons white miso paste

½ tablespoon dark soy sauce

½ tablespoon agave syrup

½ tablespoon rice vinegar

90 ml/6 tablespoons neri goma (Japanese sesame paste) (or tahini mixed with 1 tablespoon toasted sesame oil)

110 ml/½ cup dashi (Japanese stock made from bonito flakes and kombu seaweed)

1 spring onion/scallion, chopped

½ teaspoon black sesame seeds

Serves 2

In Japan, soba noodle dishes are extremely popular. They are very easy to make and a perfect example of Japanese cooking: simple yet elegant. 'Soba' means buckwheat in English, but despite the name, buckwheat contains no wheat or gluten and is really good for you.

Bring a saucepan of water to the boil and cook the soba noodles according to the packet instructions.

While they are on, bring the mirin to a fast boil in another saucepan for a minute or so to cook off the alcohol, then remove from the heat.

To make the gomadare sauce, put the sesame seeds, mirin, miso paste, soy sauce, agave syrup, rice vinegar and neri goma in a bowl and mix well. Slowly mix in the dashi, bit by bit, until you reach your desired consistency.

When the noodles are cooked, drain well and twist into a high mound on each plate with the chopped spring onion/scallion piled on top. Spoon the gomadare sauce into a little bowl beside the noodles and sprinkle the black sesame seeds on top. Serve immediately.

sweet chilli noodle salad with crunchy Asian greens

This dish is simple, fresh, extremely tasty and healthy. This noodle salad is also delicious with king prawns/shrimp or langoustines added.

3 nests of medium egg noodles

2 whole pak choi/bok choy, leaves separated

1 bunch of asparagus

50 g/2 oz. mangetout/snow peas

6 spring onions/scallions, sliced

grated zest and freshly squeezed juiced of 1 lime

1 teaspoon palm or brown sugar

1 tablespoon fish sauce

5 tablespoons sweet chilli sauce

a bunch of fresh coriander/cilantro

1 red chilli, finely sliced (optional)

Serves 4–6

Fill a saucepan three quarters full with water and bring to the boil. Add your noodles and after 2 minutes put a lidded steamer on top with the pak choi/bok choy, asparagus and mangetout/snow peas in. (If you do not have a steamer, you can cook these in a separate pan of boiling water.) Cook for a further 2 minutes (so the noodles get 4 minutes, and the greens get 2 minutes in total), then drain them together and blanch them all in cold running water. Drain again, then put both vegetables and noodles into a large mixing bowl along with the spring onions/scallions.

Combine the lime juice and zest, sugar, fish sauce and sweet chilli sauce in a small bowl to make a dressing, then fold through the noodles. Garnish with fresh coriander/cilantro and sliced chilli, if using.

peanut or sunflower oil, for deep-frying

1 packet (250 g/8 oz.) thin rice noodles

Sauce

2 tablespoons peanut or sunflower oil

125 g/4 oz. firm tofu, cut into 1-cm¼-inch cubes or thin strips

60 g/3 oz. dried shrimp

4 garlic cloves, finely chopped

4 Thai pink small shallots, or 2 regular, finely chopped

3 tablespoons Thai fish sauce

2 tablespoons palm sugar

2 tablespoons tomato sauce

4 tablespoons freshly squeezed lemon or lime juice

½ teaspoon chilli powder

Garnish

2 tablespoons peanut or sunflower oil

1 egg, lightly beaten with 1 tablespoon cold water

60 g/¾ cup beansprouts, rinsed, drained and trimmed

4 spring onions/scallions, cut into 2.5-cm/1-inch slivers

2 medium fresh red chillies, deseeded and finely sliced lengthways

2 whole heads of pickled garlic, finely sliced crossways

Serves 4

Traditional Thai meals are sharing occasions, with several dishes being prepared and presented, usually including a mix of something salty, something sweet, something crunchy and so on. This dish is seen as sweet. In the West, it has become a stand-alone snack dish. You need patience to prepare these crispy noodles, or Mee Krop, it can take quite a while to get the optimum result, but it will be well worth your time.

Thai crispy noodles

Fill a wok one-third full with the oil and heat until medium hot. Add the noodles and deep-fry until golden brown and crisp. Drain and set aside. Pour the oil into a heatproof container for another use.

Pour the oil for the sauce into the wok and fry the strips of tofu until crisp. Remove with a slotted spoon and set aside. Fry the dried shrimp until crisp. Remove with a slotted spoon and set aside.

Add the garlic to the wok, fry until golden brown, drain and set aside. Add the shallots and fry until brown. Add the fish sauce, sugar, tomato sauce and lemon juice and stir well until the mixture begins to caramelize. Add the chilli powder and the reserved tofu and garlic and stir until they have soaked up some of the liquid. Set aside.

Using a separate pan, heat the oil for the garnish and drip in the egg mixture to make little scraps of fried egg. Drain and set aside. Return the main sauce to the heat and crumble in the crispy noodles, mixing gently and briefly. Turn on to a serving dish and sprinkle with beansprouts, spring onions/scallions, fried egg scraps, chillies and pickled garlic and serve.

2 tablespoons peanut oil

1 recipe Laksa Paste (see page 10)

1.5 litres/1½ quarts chicken stock

1 stalk of lemongrass, halved lengthways

2 kaffir lime leaves (optional)

2 long sprigs of lemon balm (optional)

4 thin slices of fresh ginger or galangal

1 teaspoon light soy sauce

400 ml/1¾ cups canned coconut milk

500 g/1 lb. uncooked prawns/shrimp, shelled and deveined

125 g/1 cup beansprouts

brown sugar or palm sugar, to taste

sea salt

a bunch of fresh coriander/cilantro, chopped

To serve

a 10-cm/4 inch piece of cucumber, deseeded and sliced into matchsticks

a few lemon balm leaves, finely sliced (optional)

a handful of Chinese leaves (Chinese cabbage or Napa cabbage), shredded

Serves 4–6

laksa lemak

Laksa, the spicy prawn and noodle soup from Malaysia and Singapore, has become fashionable all over the world. This one is a speciality of the Nonya or Straits-Chinese community. Its bright yellow colour comes from turmeric and, on its home ground, fresh turmeric is often used rather than the ground turmeric found in the West. The ingredients vary according to region and what's available in the market – in Malaysia, local ingredients like the fragrant laksa leaf and wild ginger bud may also be added. A little creative licence is called for, so try the suggestions or think of your own, within reason!

Bring a saucepan of water to the boil and cook the egg noodles according to the packet instructions and drain well.

Heat the oil in a large saucepan and add the laksa paste. Sauté for about 8 minutes. Add the chicken stock, lemongrass, lime leaves, lemon balm, if using, ginger or galangal and soy sauce. Bring to the boil and add the coconut milk, stirring to keep it from separating. Reduce the heat and simmer gently for 15 minutes.

Add the prawns/shrimp, beansprouts, sugar and salt. Simmer for 2–3 minutes, until the prawns are just cooked. Discard the lemon balm and lemongrass and add the chopped coriander/cilantro.

To serve, put the noodles, cucumber, lemon balm, if using, and Chinese leaves into 4 large or 6 small bowls, then ladle in the soup.

stir-fried peanut prawns with coriander noodles

150 g/6 oz. rice stick noodles

5 tablespoons peanut oil

a pinch of ground coriander

2 kaffir lime leaves, 1 finely sliced or crushed and 1 left whole

1 stalk of lemongrass, very finely chopped

3–4 red bird's eye chillies, deseeded and finely sliced

3 spring onions/scallions, chopped

1 fat garlic clove, crushed

100 g/2 cups ready-mixed stir-fry vegetables, without beansprouts, or your choice of vegetables, all cut into bite-size pieces

a pinch of sugar

3 tablespoons Thai fish sauce

250 g/8 oz. uncooked, shelled tiger prawns, deveined (about 400 g/14 oz., shell-on)

freshly squeezed juice of 1 lemon

150 g/1 cup dry-roasted peanuts, coarsely ground

about 2 tablespoons peanut oil

25 g/¾ cup fresh coriander/cilantro, finely chopped

To serve

a handful of coriander/cilantro leaves, chopped

a few green bird's eye chillies, deseeded and finely sliced

2 spring onions/scallions, green part only, finely sliced

a handful of beansprouts

Serves 4

Similar to the popular dish, Pad Thai (see page 93), this recipe is drier, less sweet and omits certain key ingredients such as eggs, substituting stir-fry vegetables instead. Tiny, blindingly hot bird's eye chillies are an essential spice in South-east Asian cuisine: if you would prefer this dish less hot, use another kind of chilli or reduce the number.

Put the noodles into a bowl and cover with boiling water. Let soak for 4 minutes or according to the instructions on the packet. Drain, return to the bowl and cover with cold water until ready to serve. Have a kettle of boiling water ready to reheat.

Put 3 tablespoons of the oil into a non-stick wok, heat well and swirl to coat. Add the ground coriander, kaffir lime leaves, lemongrass, red chillies and chopped spring onions/scallions and stir-fry briefly. Add the garlic and stir-fry again for 20 seconds. Add the prepared vegetables, sugar and 2 tablespoons of the fish sauce and stir-fry over medium-high heat for 1 minute.

Add the prawns/shrimp and lemon juice and stir-fry for 1 minute, then add half the ground peanuts. Mix well, add the remaining tablespoon of fish sauce and cook for 2 more minutes or until the prawns turn pink.

Meanwhile, drain the noodles again and return them to the bowl. Cover with boiling water, drain and return to the bowl. Add 2 tablespoons peanut oil, toss to coat, add the coriander/cilantro and toss again. Add the noodles to the wok, toss to coat, then serve immediately topped with coriander/cilantro, green chillies, spring onions/scallions, beansprouts and the remaining peanuts.

150 g/5½ oz. dried flat Thai rice noodles

2 large garlic cloves, crushed

1 large red chilli, deseeded and finely chopped, plus ½, finely chopped, to garnish

1 teaspoon shrimp paste (optional)

1 tablespoon vegetable oil, plus extra if needed

2 skinless chicken breasts, cut into 2-cm/1-inch pieces

2 tablespoons fish sauce

2 eggs, lightly beaten

100 g/1 cup beansprouts

a small bunch of Chinese chives, cut into 4-cm/1½-inch lengths

1 tablespoon tamarind paste

1 tablespoon palm sugar or soft light brown sugar

3 tablespoons chopped roasted peanuts

2 spring onions/scallions, green and light green parts only, thinly sliced on the diagonal

a squeeze of fresh lime juice

2 tablespoons roughly chopped coriander/cilantro leaves, to garnish

lime wedges, to serve

Serves 2

Spicy and satisfying, this dish is a Thai streetfood classic. The shrimp paste adds depth to the dish, so don't let its pungent aroma put you off. And don't forget the squeeze of lime at the end for that essential tangy finish.

chicken pad Thai

Put the noodles in a large heatproof bowl and cover with boiling water. Soak for 20 minutes, or until softened but not cooked through. Drain well.

Meanwhile, put the garlic, chilli and shrimp paste, if using, in a pestle and mortar and grind until you have a rough paste. Alternatively, blitz in a food processor with a little water.

Heat the oil in a wok or large frying pan/skillet until very hot. Add the paste and fry over high heat for 1 minute, or until fragrant. Season the chicken with ½ tablespoon of the fish sauce and add to the wok. Stir-fry for 4 minutes, or until just cooked through. Remove the chicken from the wok and set aside.

Heat another ½ tablespoon oil in the wok, if necessary. When hot, pour in the beaten eggs. Leave the bottom to set, then break up with a spoon to get softly set scrambled eggs. Return the chicken to the wok with the noodles, beansprouts and chives. Stir well.

Meanwhile, combine the remaining fish sauce with the tamarind paste and palm sugar, then add to the wok with half the peanuts. Stir-fry for 2–4 minutes, or until the noodles are tender. You may need to sprinkle in a little water if the noodles look too dry. Stir in the spring onions/scallions and lime juice. Taste and add more fish sauce if you think it needs it.

Divide the pad Thai between 2 bowls, garnish with the fresh coriander/cilantro leaves, chilli and remaining peanuts, and serve immediately with lime wedges.

Indonesian fried rice

Sambal olek is a concentrated chilli paste with a fiery kick. It is often used to enliven Indonesian dishes such as this punchy meat and vegetable fried rice and can be increased or reduced in quantity, depending on how much heat you like.

2½ tablespoons vegetable oil

1 small onion, finely chopped

2 garlic cloves, crushed

2 tablespoons sambal olek or chilli sauce

2 teaspoons shrimp paste

1 large skinless chicken breast, about 220 g/8 oz., diced

200 g/6½ oz. uncooked shelled prawns/shrimp, roughly chopped

100 g/3½ oz. carrot, finely grated

200 g/6½ oz. canned sweetcorn/corn, well drained

100 g/3½ oz. trimmed green beans, finely chopped

500 g/1 lb. cold, cooked basmati rice

1 tablespoon light soy sauce

2 large eggs, lightly beaten with a pinch of sea salt

Serves 4

Heat 2 tablespoons of the oil in a wok or large frying pan/skillet until hot. Add the onion and stir-fry over high heat for 2–3 minutes, or until softened and golden. Add the garlic and continue to cook for 1 minute. Add the sambal olek and shrimp paste and cook for 1 minute, then throw in the chicken. Stir-fry for 2 minutes, then add the prawns/shrimp and cook until opaque and just cooked through.

Throw in the carrot, sweetcorn/corn and green beans and cook for about 2 minutes, or until the beans are cooked but still crunchy.

Add the rice and soy sauce to the wok and mix through. Cook until the rice is piping hot, then remove from the heat and set aside.

Heat the remaining oil in a large frying pan/skillet and pour in the beaten eggs. Leave to set into a thin omelette. Transfer to a wooden board and leave to cool for 1 minute. Roll up the omelette tightly and slice as thinly as possible.

Divide the fried rice between 4 bowls and garnish with the slices of omelette.

1½ tablespoons vegetable oil

2 small shallots, halved and thinly sliced

2 garlic cloves, crushed

a 3-cm/1-inch piece of fresh ginger, peeled and finely grated

1 red chilli, deseeded and finely chopped

1 lemongrass stalk, outer skin removed and bottom 10 cm/ 4 inches finely chopped

350 g/12 oz. minced/ground pork

3½ tablespoons fish sauce

2 tablespoons Chinese rice wine or dry sherry

3 tablespoons chilli sauce

freshly squeezed juice of 1 lime

3½ tablespoons honey

200 g/6½ oz. dried glass or cellophane noodles

a small bunch of coriander/cilantro leaves, roughly chopped

4 large iceberg lettuce leaves

120 g/¾ cup honey-roasted peanuts, roughly chopped

Serves 4

This refreshing salad gets its heat from the chilli sauce and fresh ginger, sweetness from honey, tartness from lime juice and saltiness from roasted peanuts. It is made with distinctive transparent glass noodles. Serve this dish as a light summer starter for four people, or for two as a sumptuous main course.

Laotian pork and glass noodle salad

Heat the oil in a wok or large frying pan/skillet until hot. Throw in the shallots and stir-fry over high heat for 2 minutes. Add the garlic, ginger, chilli and lemongrass. Cook for 2 more minutes until the garlic is golden.

Add the pork and stir to break up any lumps. Stir-fry until browned, then add the fish sauce, rice wine, chilli sauce, lime juice and honey. Simmer for 2 minutes, then remove from the heat.

Meanwhile, put the noodles in a large heatproof bowl and cover with boiling water. Soak for 3–4 minutes, or until softened. Drain and rinse under cold running water. Cut them into shorter strands with kitchen scissors.

Add the noodles to the wok and mix evenly through the pork mixture. Return to the heat and simmer for 3–4 minutes, or until the noodles have absorbed most of the liquid. Remove from the heat and stir in the chopped coriander/cilantro.

You can serve the salad hot, or leave it to cool to room temperature, then chill in the fridge for a few hours first. Serve in the lettuce leaves and garnish with the chopped peanuts.

400 g/14 oz. fillet steak/beef tenderloin

1 tablespoon sunflower oil

100 g/3½ oz. bamboo shoots, finely shredded

100 g/⅔ cup roasted salted peanuts, coarsely ground

200 g/6½ oz. baby spinach leaves

500 g/1 lb. thin rice noodles

1 teaspoon toasted sesame oil

8 spring onions/scallions, thinly sliced

3 tablespoons Nuóc Cham (see page 19)

2 handfuls of fresh coriander/cilantro, finely chopped

2–3 baby courgettes/zucchini (about 200 g/6½ oz.), sliced into ribbons with a mandolin or potato slicer

freshly squeezed juice of ½ lime

a pinch of salt

2 thin red chillies, very thinly sliced

Marinade

1 lemongrass stick, very finely chopped

2 teaspoons Thai red curry paste

2 teaspoons nam pla fish sauce

freshly squeezed juice of ½ lime

Serves 4

Thai-spiced rare beef and warm rice noodle salad

This recipe makes a deliciously different and tasty oriental variation on a simple salad.

To make the marinade, mix the lemongrass, curry paste, fish sauce and lime juice, then place the beef in a shallow dish and cover with the marinade. Cover and refrigerate.

Heat the oil in a frying pan/skillet over medium heat and fry the marinated beef (reserving any remaining marinade) for 2 minutes each side. Remove from the pan, cover and set aside. In the same pan, quickly fry the bamboo shoots and peanuts with any remaining marinade. Add the spinach to the pan, immediately remove from the heat and cover with a lid to allow the spinach to wilt in the residual heat.

Blanch the noodles in a pan of boiling water for 5 minutes or until cooked. Drain and toss in the sesame oil, spring onions/scallions, Nuóc Cham and half the coriander/cilantro. Meanwhile, thinly slice the beef and keep warm.

Dress the courgettes/zucchini with the lime juice, the remaining coriander/cilantro and the salt.

To serve, divide the noodles between 4 warm plates, then pile the remaining ingredients on top. Garnish with the sliced chillies.

japchae with sweet potato noodles

150 g/5 oz. beef, thinly sliced, eg. sirloin (omit if you are vegetarian)

10 shiitake mushrooms, sliced

dark soy sauce

toasted sesame oil

agave syrup

1 garlic clove, smashed

150 g/5 oz. spinach leaves

250 g/8 oz. cellophane noodles (made from sweet potato starch)

vegetable oil

100 g/3½ oz. carrot, cut into thin matchsticks

1 large red onion, sliced

1 tablespoon chilli paste (try to find authentic Korean gochujang paste in Asian stores)

1 tablespoon sesame seeds, lightly toasted

1 egg

black sesame seeds and sliced chilli, to serve

kimchi, to serve (Korean fermented cabbage)

Serves 6

Korean food is extremely healthy and full of flavour. This dish is naturally sugar, wheat and dairy free – even the noodles, which are made from sweet potatoes.

Put the beef, mushrooms, 1 tablespoon soy sauce, 1 tablespoon sesame oil, 1 tablespoon agave syrup and the garlic in a bowl, make sure the beef and mushrooms are well coated and marinate for 15 minutes or a few hours if you have time.

Meanwhile, rinse the spinach, then drain and put straight into a large saucepan over high heat. Watch over it as it wilts very quickly, and stir often. Remove to a sieve/strainer and press the remaining water out of it. Put on a plate while still warm and season with a little soy sauce and sesame oil.

Cook the noodles in a large pan of boiling, salted water for 6 minutes or until tender. While they are cooking, stir-fry the beef and mushrooms with a little vegetable oil in a separate pan. Do the same with the carrot and onion until just tender and slightly coloured, then drizzle over a little sesame oil and soy sauce.

Mix together 3 tablespoons each soy sauce and agave syrup, the chilli paste and 2½ tablespoons sesame oil.

Drain the cooked noodles well, then return to the empty pan. Add the fried vegetables, chilli sauce and sesame seeds. Crack the egg on top and, over medium heat, toss everything together until evenly mixed and the egg is cooked. It may need another dash of sesame, soy or agave depending on your tastes but don't get carried away, as they are strong flavours. Serve immediately with black sesame seeds and sliced chilli scattered over, and kimchi on the side, if you like.

Heat up a wok or large frying pan/skillet and stir-fry your way to a meal in minutes with this collection of recipes. Serve on a bed of rice, noodles or even a mound of wasabi mash and you'll have a delicious dinner fit for any occasion.

main dishes

Buddha's delight

½ teaspoon Chinese five-spice powder (see page 12)

250 g/8 oz. firm tofu, cut into 2-cm/1-inch cubes

2 tablespoons vegetable oil

3 garlic cloves, crushed

200 g/6½ oz. small broccoli florets

200 g/6½ oz. miniature or baby pak choi/bok choy, halved

200 g/6½ oz. mangetout/snow peas

1 large carrot, cut into matchsticks

1 red (bell) pepper, deseeded and cut into matchsticks

85 g/3 oz. canned water chestnuts, drained and sliced

85 g/3 oz. canned sliced bamboo shoots, drained and rinsed

Sauce

2 tablespoons oyster sauce

2 tablespoons light soy sauce

125 ml/½ cup vegetable stock

1 tablespoon cornflour/cornstarch, combined with 2 tablespoons cold water

Serves 4

This is a hearty and flavoursome vegetarian dish traditionally eaten on the first day of Chinese New Year – Buddhists believe that meat should not be eaten on the first five days of the year. Every Buddhist family has their own version and ingredients vary from cook to cook.

Combine all the sauce ingredients in a bowl and set aside.

Sprinkle the five-spice powder over the tofu.

Heat the oil in a wok or large frying pan/skillet until hot. Add the tofu in batches and stir-fry over high heat until golden all over. Remove the tofu from the wok and drain well on paper towels.

Add the garlic to the wok and stir-fry for 1 minute, or until golden. Add the broccoli, pak choi/bok choy, mangetout/snow peas, carrot and red (bell) pepper with a sprinkle of water and stir-fry over high heat for 2–3 minutes. Finally, throw in the water chestnuts and bamboo shoots.

Pour the sauce into the wok and bring to the boil, then reduce the heat and simmer gently for 2 minutes, or until the sauce has thickened. Divide between 4 bowls and serve.

3 tablespoons dark soy sauce

toasted sesame oil

1 teaspoon agave syrup

freshly squeezed juice of 1 lime

2 salmon fillets

500 g/1 lb. potatoes

sea salt

100 g/3½ oz. pak choi/bok choy, halved lengthways if fat

extra virgin olive oil

100 ml/6 tablespoons soy cream/creamer

1 spring onion/scallion

wasabi paste or powder

1 teaspoon sesame seeds, toasted

Serves 2

The heat of wasabi is a wonderful way to liven up mashed potatoes, and the flavour goes so well with soy- and sesame-marinated salmon.

soy salmon, wasabi mash and pak choi

Mix together the soy sauce, 1 tablespoon sesame oil, the agave syrup and lime juice in a resealable bag. Place the salmon fillets inside, seal the bag and marinate for at least 20 minutes, or for a few hours if you have the time.

Put the potatoes in a saucepan of cold, salted water. Bring to the boil and cook until just tender but not falling apart. While the potatoes are cooking, bring another pan of water to the boil, add a good pinch of salt and cook the pak choi/bok choy for a few minutes until they are just tender but still have a bit of bite. Drain and season with a drizzle of olive oil and a few drops of sesame oil. Keep warm.

When the potatoes are cooked, drain and place a dry dish towel on top to absorb any remaining moisture. After a few minutes, peel the potatoes by just pulling off the skin. Add the soy cream/creamer, plenty of olive oil and the spring onion/scallion and mash until smooth. You may need more oil as it really does soak in. Season to taste with salt, then cautiously add some wasabi paste or powder. It should be strong enough to definitely taste it though.

When the potatoes are mashed, heat a dry frying pan/skillet over medium heat and add the salmon fillets (reserving the marinade). Fry for 3–4 minutes, then flip over and fry until just cooked through. A minute or so before it is done, add the remaining marinade. Let it bubble, then remove from the heat.

Plate up the mash, place the salmon on top and nestle the pak choi/bok choy on top. Sprinkle over some sesame seeds and enjoy.

quick-fried teriyaki salmon with bok choi

650 g/1½ lbs. skinless salmon fillet, cut into 2-cm/1-inch pieces

1 tablespoon vegetable oil

3 spring onions/scallions, white and light green parts only, thinly sliced on the diagonal

350 g/12 oz. miniature or baby pak choi/bok choy, leaves thickly sliced and stalks thinly sliced

Marinade

1 tablespoon finely grated fresh ginger

3 tablespoons shoyu or tamari soy sauce (or light soy sauce)

3 tablespoons mirin (Japanese rice wine)

2 tablespoons honey

Serves 4

This is a great prepare-ahead weekday supper – simply marinate the salmon with a gingery, honeyed teriyaki sauce the night before, then stir-fry with crunchy pak-choi for a nutritious and delicious meal in under 15 minutes.

Combine all the marinade ingredients in a bowl, then add the salmon pieces and mix well. Cover and marinate in the fridge overnight, if possible, or for 10–15 minutes.

Heat the oil in a wok or large frying pan/skillet until hot, then add the salmon in 2 batches – shake off as much marinade as possible and reserve the marinade. Stir-fry the salmon over high heat for about 3 minutes, stirring occasionally, until sealed all over but the inside is still a little pink. Remove the salmon from the wok and set aside.

Add the spring onions/scallions to the wok and stir-fry for 30 seconds. Add the pak choi/bok choy and stir-fry for 1 minute, then add the reserved marinade and cook for 1 minute, stirring, until the leaves have just wilted and the stalks are cooked through but still crunchy. Return the salmon to the wok and gently stir through.

Divide between 4 bowls and serve.

cod with black bean sauce

Pungent black bean sauce pairs beautifully with the subtle taste of cod in this simple, authentic recipe. Remember not to be too heavy-handed with the black bean sauce, as a little goes a long way. Feel free to substitute the cod with any other firm white fish.

1 tablespoon peanut oil

1 shallot, thinly sliced

2 garlic cloves, thinly sliced

a 2-cm/1-inch piece of fresh ginger, peeled and shredded

2 spring onions/scallions, thinly sliced, white and green parts kept separately

1½ tablespoons black bean sauce

90 ml/⅓ cup fish stock

1 teaspoon sugar

380 g/12 oz. cod fillets, cut into 3-cm/1¼-inch pieces

1 teaspoon toasted sesame oil, to serve

Serves 2

Heat the oil in a wok or large frying pan/skillet until hot, then add the shallot, garlic, ginger and white parts of the spring onions/scallions. Stir-fry over high heat for 2 minutes, then stir in the black bean sauce.

Pour in the stock, along with the sugar, and bring to the boil. Simmer rapidly for 2 minutes until thickened, then reduce the heat and add the cod. Cook for about 3 minutes, stirring occasionally, until the fish is cooked through.

Divide between 2 bowls and serve with rice. Drizzle over the sesame oil and garnish with the green parts of the spring onions/scallions.

1 sea bass, about 1 kg/1 lb.

peanut or sunflower oil, for frying

Sweet and sour topping

2 teaspoons cornflour/starch

2 tablespoons peanut or sunflower oil

2 garlic cloves, finely chopped

100 g/½ cup pineapple chunks, fresh or canned

a 8-cm/3-inch piece of cucumber, quartered lengthways, then thickly sliced crossways

1 small onion, halved, then sliced into thin segments

2 small tomatoes, quartered

3 medium spring onions/scallions, coarsely chopped into 2.5-cm/ 1-inch lengths

2 large fresh red chillies, sliced diagonally

2 tablespoons Thai fish sauce

1 tablespoon light soy sauce

1 teaspoon sugar

½ teaspoon freshly ground white pepper

Serves 4

The sweet and sour topping from this dish can be adapted to suit vegetarians. Instead of fish sauce, use extra soy sauce, then serve with rice and other vegetarian dishes.

sweet and sour fish

Make a diagonal cut in each side of the fish.

Fill a wok or deep-fryer one-third full with the oil or to the manufacturer's recommended level. Heat until a scrap of noodle will puff up immediately.

Add the fish and fry until golden and crispy. Remove from the oil, drain and put on a serving dish.

Mix the cornflour/cornstarch with 5 tablespoons water in a small cup and set aside.

Heat the oil in a wok or deep frying pan/skillet, add the garlic and fry until golden brown. Stirring constantly, add the pineapple, cucumber, onion, tomatoes, spring onions/scallions, chillies, fish sauce, soy sauce, sugar and pepper.

Stir the cornflour/starch mixture to loosen it, then add to the vegetables and stir briefly to thicken the sauce. Pour over the fish, then serve.

8 skinless chicken thighs (bone in), each cut into 3 with a sharp cleaver

2 tablespoons peanut oil

1 onion, very thinly sliced

3 bird's-eye chillies, chopped, plus extra, shredded, to garnish (optional)

3 tablespoons fish sauce

1 teaspoon sugar

lime wedges, to serve

3 spring onions/scallions, green and light green parts only, thinly sliced on the diagonal, to garnish

Marinade

1 tablespoon finely grated fresh ginger

3 garlic cloves, crushed

3 lemongrass stalks, outer skin removed, cut into 2-cm/1-inch pieces and well bruised

5 fresh kaffir lime leaves, torn to release their aroma

sea salt

Serves 4

Fresh lemongrass and kaffir lime leaves infuse this Vietnamese-style dish with a tantalizing citrus zing. Using skinless chicken thighs keeps the stir-fry moist without unnecessary fat and with the bone in you get lots more flavour from the chicken.

Vietnamese fried chicken

Combine the marinade ingredients in a bowl with a good sprinkling of salt. Stir in the chicken, cover and marinate in the fridge for 20–30 minutes.

Heat the oil in a wok or large frying pan/skillet until very hot, then add the chicken in 2 batches. Stir-fry over high heat for 5 minutes, or until the chicken is golden all over. Remove the chicken from the wok and set aside.

Add the onion and chillies to the wok and stir-fry for 1 minute. Return all the chicken to the wok with the fish sauce and sugar and toss everything together. Reduce the heat and continue to stir-fry for 5 minutes, or until the chicken is cooked through. Taste and add more fish sauce if you think it needs it.

Divide between 4 bowls and serve with rice and lime wedges. Garnish with the spring onions/scallions and shredded chillies, if using.

red-cooked chicken legs

150 ml/⅔ cups dark soy sauce

3 tablespoons Chinese rice wine or dry sherry

2 thin slices of fresh ginger

3 cinnamon sticks, halved

5 whole star anise

2 whole cloves

3 spring onions/scallions

½ teaspoon grated orange or lemon zest

1 tablespoon fresh lemon juice

½ teaspoon sugar

4 large chicken legs (thighs and drumsticks)

Serves 4

Chinese red-cooking involves poaching meat, poultry, game, offal or even fish in a dark, soy-based sauce. When the sauce is spiced with star anise, cinnamon and sometimes additional spices from the five-spice brigade, it is used as a 'master sauce'. You will sometimes find spices such as liquorice root and citrus peel in a master sauce as well, depending on the dish. Master sauce is used like a stock, cooked first as in the recipe below, then stored for later use. When it has been used a few times, it is considered mature and more desirable. Serve with rice or a noodle dish, stir-fried vegetables and other Chinese dishes.

Add the ginger, cinnamon, star anise, cloves, spring onions/scallions, orange or lemon zest, lemon juice and sugar. Bring to the boil and turn off the heat. Leave for at least 10 minutes to infuse the flavours.

Add the chicken legs and bring to the boil. Reduce the heat and simmer for 40 minutes, or until cooked through and tender.

Transfer the legs to a serving bowl or plate and spoon over some of the sauce. Alternatively, use a Chinese cleaver to chop them into bite-size pieces. Transfer any remaining sauce to an airtight container and refrigerate (or freeze) for later use.

Thai green chicken curry

This famous Thai curry is full of the fragrance of fresh spices and herbs for which Thai cuisine is known. Coconut milk tempers the heat of the tiny bird's eye chillies in the green curry paste (although this is a mild version) and adds the essential creaminess. Throughout South-east Asia, although dried spices are certainly used, the fresh versions are more typical. The spice trade grew out of the desire, especially in Europe, for the flavours of Asian spices. These were mostly used fresh in their own countries, but they could only be exported in their dry form. Modern modes of transport and polytunnel agriculture mean that fresh chillies, ginger and similar spices are available in almost every supermarket.

800 ml/3½ cups canned coconut milk

1 recipe Thai Green Curry Paste (see page 11) or 7 tablespoons store-bought paste

4 boneless skinless chicken breasts, preferably free-range or organic, thickly sliced

2 tablespoons Thai fish sauce

¼ teaspoon brown sugar or palm sugar

To serve

Thai basil leaves or chopped coriander/cilantro

1 lime, cut into 4 wedges

3 bird's eye chillies, halved lengthways (optional)

Serves 4

Put a ladle of the the coconut milk into a wok or deep frying pan/skillet, add the curry paste and stir-fry to release the aromas. Add the chicken and stir-fry to coat with the spices. Add the remaining coconut milk, bring to the boil, reduce the heat and gently simmer for about 8 minutes, or until the chicken is cooked through and still tender.

Add the fish sauce and sugar and cook for a further 1 minute. Transfer to a serving bowl, sprinkle with the herbs, add the lime wedges and serve.

2 large skinless chicken breasts, cut into 2-cm/1-inch pieces

1 tablespoon peanut oil

1 red (bell) pepper, deseeded and thinly sliced

1 yellow pepper, deseeded and thinly sliced

2 tablespoons yellow bean sauce

½ tablespoon light soy sauce

70 ml/⅓ cup chicken stock

2 teaspoons cornflour/cornstarch

1 tablespoon flaked/slivered almonds, lightly toasted, to garnish (optional)

Marinade

½ tablespoon Chinese rice wine or dry sherry

1 tablespoon light soy sauce

1 teaspoon toasted sesame oil

½ teaspoon sugar

1 teaspoon finely grated fresh ginger

a pinch of dried chilli/red pepper flakes

Serves 2

chicken with yellow bean sauce and rainbow peppers

Ideal for quick and casual entertaining, this isn't just a routine stir-fry – the distinctive savoury taste of yellow bean sauce and the colourful combination of red and yellow peppers make for a memorable dish.

Combine all the marinade ingredients in a bowl, then add the chicken pieces and mix well. Cover and marinate in the fridge for 10–15 minutes.

Heat the oil in a wok or large frying pan/skillet until hot, then add the chicken and stir-fry over high heat for 3–4 minutes until golden, well sealed and nearly cooked through. Remove from the wok and set aside.

Add the peppers to the wok and stir-fry over high heat for 2 minutes. Return the chicken to the wok and add the yellow bean sauce. Cook for 1 minute, stirring occasionally.

Meanwhile, combine the soy sauce, stock and cornflour/cornstarch in a bowl with 2 tablespoons cold water. Stir until smooth, then pour into the wok. Simmer gently until the sauce has thickened and the chicken is cooked through.

Divide between 2 bowls and sprinkle with almonds, if using, to garnish.

Thai herbs and spices are delicious with delicate quail. Grill them or roast them in the oven. Either way, they are crispy brown and bursting with flavour. Serve with a bowl of jasmine rice with the quail propped on top, with juicy lime wedges to squeeze.

Thai lemongrass quail

8 quail, halved lengthwise along the backbones

1 recipe of Thai Lemongrass Paste (see page 9)

6 limes, quartered, to serve

Serves 4

Rinse the quail under cold water and pat dry with a paper towel. Put them in a ceramic baking dish and pour over the Thai Lemongrass Paste. Rub the paste into the quail on both sides, then cover and refrigerate for 6–8 hours, or overnight.

After this time, remove the quail from the fridge and leave to come up to room temperature.

Preheat a gas or charcoal grill/barbecue or a grill pan on the stove top over a medium–high heat.

Lay the quail on the heated grill/barbecue, skin side down, and cook for 8 minutes per side until cooked through. When done, remove from the grill, cover, and let stand for 10 minutes.

Serve the quail with lime wedges for squeezing over.

grilled duck with tamarind sauce

4 duck breasts, with or without skin

3 tablespoons Thai fish sauce

2 large red chillies, cut into small strips

coriander/cilantro leaves, to serve

Duck marinade

4 garlic cloves, finely chopped

1 tablespoon finely chopped coriander/cilantro root

1 teaspoon ground cumin

2 tablespoons Thai fish sauce

1 tablespoon light soy sauce

2 teaspoons sugar

Tamarind sauce

2 tablespoons peanut or sunflower oil

2 large garlic cloves, finely chopped

1 tablespoon grated fresh ginger

2 tablespoons tamarind water

2 tablespoons vegetable stock or water

2 tablespoons sugar

Serves 4

This dish is a combination of Thai and Chinese cuisines. Duck is not a traditional ingredient in Thai cooking, so when it does appear it is often cooked using roast duck prepared in the Chinese style. For this recipe, the key ingredient is the tamarind water.

To make the marinade, put the garlic, coriander/cilantro root, cumin, fish sauce, soy sauce and sugar in a bowl and mix well. Add the duck, coating it well with the mixture, and leave to marinate for 1 hour.

When ready to cook, remove the duck from the marinade and pat it dry with paper towels. Preheat the grill/broiler to a high heat and cook the duck for 5 minutes on each side, then slice diagonally and set aside.

To make the tamarind sauce, heat the oil in a wok or frying pan/skillet, add the garlic and fry until golden. Add the ginger, tamarind water, stock and sugar, stirring well. Add the sliced duck and sprinkle with fish sauce and strips of chilli, stirring well. Transfer to a serving dish, top with coriander/cilantro and serve.

*Note To prepare your own tamarind water, mix 1 tablespoon tamarind pulp in a bowl with 150ml/⅔ cup hot water, mashing with a fork. As you mix the pulp and water, the water absorbs the taste of the tamarind. When the water is cool, you can squeeze the tamarind pulp to extract more juice (and remove any seeds). Pour off the juice in to a container and set aside for use in recipes. It will keep for about a week in the refrigerator.

fermented black bean pork with peaches

Let your eyes feast on this beautiful dish of ripe peaches with dark fermented black beans. Of course, summer is the best time for peaches, but don't be put off if you want to make it any other time – just select a seasonal fruit that will compliment the pork and the saltiness of the beans.

2 pork fillets/tenderloins (weighing about 680 g/1½ lb. in total)

1 recipe of Fermented Black Bean Paste (see page 9)

4 ripe peaches

2 tablespoons orange blossom honey

vegetable oil, for searing

4 limes, quartered, to serve

Serves 4–6

Wash the pork under cold water and pat dry with a paper towel. Put the pork in a ceramic baking dish, pour over the Fermented Black Bean Paste and rub into the pork. Cover and refrigerate for 6–24 hours.

After this time, remove the marinated pork from the fridge and let it come to room temperature.

Preheat the oven to 190°C (375°F) Gas 5.

Cut the peaches into quarters and place them in a glass or ceramic bowl. Pour over the honey and toss to coat. Set aside.

Heat an ovenproof sauté pan over a medium–high heat. Remove the pork from the marinade and shake off any excess sauce. Drizzle the pan with a little vegetable oil and sear the pork on all sides.

Pour the remaining marinade into the pan and arrange the peaches around the pork. Transfer the pan to the preheated oven and roast the pork for 15–20 minutes. When done, remove from the oven, cover, and leave to rest for 10 minutes.

Slice the pork crosswise and serve in bowls with the sauce and peaches, and wedges of fresh lime.

3 tablespoons peanut or vegetable oil

750 g/1½ lb. well trimmed boneless pork sparerib, sliced into chunks

500 ml/2 cups beef stock

Hinleh (curry) paste

4–6 red bird's eye chillies, deseeded and chopped

5 garlic cloves, quartered

½ onion, coarsely chopped

a 5-cm/2-inch piece of fresh ginger, peeled and grated

¼ teaspoon ground turmeric

a 2-cm/1-inch piece of fresh galangal, peeled and grated

1 stalk of lemongrass, outer leaves discarded, the remainder very finely chopped

3 anchovies in oil, drained and finely chopped plus a dash of fish sauce, or ½ teaspoon dried shrimp paste, toasted

To serve

a handful of Thai basil or coriander/cilantro

2 red bird's eye chillies, finely sliced lengthways

Serves 4

This curry is a Burmese speciality and doesn't include the coconut milk so typical of South-east Asian cooking. It does use three root spices from the same family – turmeric, ginger and galangal. In Burma and throughout Asia, all three are used fresh, but in the West, turmeric is rarely available fresh, so the ground form must be used instead. If you can't get fresh galangal, use extra fresh ginger instead (a pity, because galangal's bright flavour is delicious).

Burmese pork hinleh

To make the hinleh paste, put all the ingredients into a blender and grind to a paste, adding a dash of water to let the blades run. Alternatively, use a mortar and pestle.

Heat the oil in a large saucepan and add the paste. Stir-fry for several minutes. Add the pork and stir-fry to seal. Add the stock, bring to the boil, reduce the heat and simmer gently, stirring occasionally, for 40–45 minutes until cooked through but very tender. Sprinkle with the herbs and chilli and serve.

pork with chilli, Thai sweet basil and toasted coconut

4–5 tablespoons grated fresh coconut (or desiccated, if necessary)

600 g/1 lb. 4 oz. pork fillet/tenderloin

2 tablespoons vegetable oil

a 3-cm/1-inch piece of fresh ginger

3 garlic cloves, thinly sliced

4 whole bird's-eye chillies

1 lemongrass stalk, outer skin removed and bottom 6 cm/ 2 inches bruised

1 tablespoon fish sauce

2 tablespoons chilli sauce

a large handful of Thai sweet basil

sea salt and freshly ground black pepper

Serves 4

Pork fillet is given a spicy boost with classic Thai flavourings and the toasted coconut finishes off this super-tasty stir-fry perfectly. If you can't get hold of Thai sweet basil, simply replace with coriander/cilantro.

Heat a wok or large frying pan/skillet until hot. Add the coconut and dry-fry over high heat for a few minutes until golden. Remove from the wok and set aside.

Put the pork fillet/tenderloin between 2 large sheets of clingfilm/plastic wrap and hit with a rolling pin until you have flattened it to about 2 cm/1 inch. Slice very thinly and season with sea salt and black pepper.

Heat the oil in a wok or large frying pan until hot, then sear the pork in 2 or 3 batches over high heat, adding more oil if necessary. Remove the pork from the wok and set aside.

Add the ginger, garlic, chillies and lemongrass to the wok and stir-fry for 1 minute. Return the pork to the wok and stir for 1 minute. Add the fish sauce and chilli sauce and stir well. Cook for 2 minutes, or until the pork is completely cooked through. Remove from the heat and stir in the Thai sweet basil.

Divide between 4 bowls and serve immediately, garnished with the toasted coconut.

sweet and sour pork with pineapple and cucumber

A world away from the local takeout's greasy battered nuggets drowned in a fluorescent gloop, this scrumptious recipe uses lean pork fillet, wok-fried with cucumber wedges and juicy pineapple chunks and lightly coated in a sweet and tangy sauce.

600 g/1 lb. 4 oz. pork fillet/tenderloin, cut into 2-cm/1-inch chunks

1 tablespoon light soy sauce

2 teaspoons finely grated fresh ginger

2 tablespoons vegetable oil

1 large red (bell) pepper, deseeded and cut into 2-cm/1-inch chunks

1 large onion, cut into 8 wedges

½ large cucumber, roughly peeled, halved, deseeded and thickly sliced

300 g/10 oz. fresh or canned pineapple, cut into 2-cm/1-inch chunks

Sauce

100 ml/⅓ cup pure pineapple juice

4 tablespoons tomato ketchup

2 tablespoons rice vinegar

1 tablespoon light soy sauce

1 tablespoon sugar

1 tablespoon cornflour/starch

Serves 4

Combine all the sauce ingredients in a bowl and set aside.

Put the pork, soy sauce and ginger in a bowl and mix well. Cover and marinate in the fridge for 20 minutes, if possible.

Heat the oil in a wok or large frying pan/skillet until hot, then add the pork in batches (don't over-crowd the wok, otherwise the pork will stew rather than fry). Stir-fry over high heat for 4–5 minutes until nearly cooked through and well sealed all over. Remove the pork from the wok and set aside.

Throw the red (bell) pepper and onion into the wok and stir-fry for 2–3 minutes. Return the pork to the wok with any juices. Pour in the sauce and toss everything together. Bring to the boil, then reduce the heat. Add the cucumber and pineapple and simmer gently for 3–4 minutes, or until the sauce has thickened and the pork is cooked through.

Divide between 4 bowls and serve immediately.

An easy dish to prepare and cook, this is a suitable recipe for those new to Thai cooking. The combination of garlic and chilli ensures a very hot and traditional Thai flavour.

pork with garlic and fresh chilli

2 tablespoons peanut or sunflower oil

3 large garlic cloves, finely chopped

500 g/1 lb. lean pork, finely sliced

2 tablespoons Thai fish sauce

2 tablespoons light soy sauce

2 large fresh red chillies, finely sliced

2 spring onions/scallions, finely sliced, to serve

Serves 4

Heat the oil in a wok or frying pan/skillet until a light haze appears. Add the garlic and stir-fry until golden brown. Add the pork and stir-fry briefly.

Add the fish sauce, soy sauce and chillies, stirring all the time. By now the pork should be cooked through. Spoon onto a serving dish and top with the sliced spring onions/scallions.

tamarind lamb with sugar snap peas

400 g/14 oz. lamb leg steaks, cut into 2-cm/1-inch cubes

1½ tablespoons vegetable oil

160 g/1½ cups sugar snap peas

Marinade

2½ tablespoons tamarind paste

3 tablespoons freshly squeezed orange juice

2½ tablespoons palm sugar or soft dark brown sugar

1 teaspoon finely grated fresh ginger

1 red chilli, deseeded and finely chopped

1 garlic clove, crushed

½ teaspoon sea salt, plus extra if needed

Serves 2

Tamarind fruits contain a soft, sticky pulp with a tart, mouth-puckering taste. The pulp is widely used in Asian cooking and is conveniently available in paste form in jars. In this recipe, toffee-like palm sugar balances the sour tamarind and gives a wonderful depth to the dish.

Combine all the marinade ingredients in a non-metal bowl, stir in the lamb, cover and marinate in the fridge for 30–60 minutes. Bring up to room temperature before cooking.

Remove the lamb from the bowl of marinade, letting any excess marinade drip from the meat back into the bowl. Heat the oil in a wok or large frying pan/skillet until hot, then stir-fry the lamb in 2 or 3 batches over high heat until sealed all over. Return all the lamb to the wok, reduce the heat and stir in the sugar snap peas.

Pour in the reserved marinade and simmer gently until the sugar snap peas are cooked through but still crunchy. Taste and add more salt if you think it needs it.

Divide between 2 bowls and serve.